BUDGETING

The Limitless Wealth Building Power of the
Compound Effect

(Easy Steps Learn How to Go From Broke to the
Bank)

Merlin Seifert

Published by Alex Howard

Merlin Seifert

All Rights Reserved

Budgeting: The Limitless Wealth Building Power of the Compound Effect (Easy Steps Learn How to Go From Broke to the Bank)

ISBN 978-1-77485-066-4

Legal & Disclaimer

Table of Contents

Introduction

Many people are lured into the trap of spending more money each week than they are bringing in and most people are doing this without even realizing it. The main reason this happens is because we are no longer taught or remember how to budget our money. With the introduction of credit, it has become easier to use money that you don't actually have.

This lack of money budgeting in today's world is beginning to reach a cataclysm with many families and individuals who are now finding themselves with severe debt problems and little knowledge about how to turn their bleak situation around. Even with all of the bad debt write-offs, banks are more than happy with the way things are. Banks build in their own risk factors based on bad debt in their interest rates to give them profit regardless of bad debt write-offs. Simply put, those borrowing money are paying for their inability to budget effectively.

Many people get so used to luxuries, they turn these things into fixtures in their weekly, fortnightly or monthly spending habits. By weeding these expenses out or making them a luxury again which is only enjoyed occasionally, you can also save quite a substantial amount of money.

When you go through your spending habits, you will be able to calculate how much you are actually spending on these things. Money budgeting is about your personal set of circumstances and your personal finances, not someone else's. Just because your neighbors have just bought the latest car model or had cable television installed, doesn't mean that you have to the same. Pay attention to your budget and let it be your decider on whether you can afford the things that you want.

Budgeting is a vital skill needed to control your finances and avoid getting into serious debt. By educating yourself on how to budget effectively, taking the time to carefully plan a good budget and monitoring it regularly you will be able to keep yourself and your family encouraged to stick with it.

Set achievable goals and even though, at first, money budgeting may seem tough, it is the only way to have the things that you want, as well as a secure financial future.

Thanks again for downloading this book. I hope you enjoy it!

Now, let's get started.

Chapter 1: Budgeting

Common people only budget their money when they are short of funds. Financially successful people do it all the time.

Budgeting includes all the spending techniques that we apply to ensure that we spend less money than we receive. For most people, budgeting means making their current cash balance fit for all their needs and their wants until the next payday. Wiser people use budgeting as a way to prepare for the future and to reach their saving goals.

Budgeting's negative reputation

Because people tend to do budgeting only when they are low on cash, it creates a negative feeling in them. They feel bad when they follow a budget because it feels like that they are depriving themselves of the good things and experiences. They feel that they deserve to spend their own money any way they want. They want to gain good feelings from the money they worked hard for and budgeting prevents them from doing that.

It is challenging to ask the people around you to follow a budget. The more you force people to limit their personal rewards, the more they want to spend. If you want your entire household to follow a budget, you need to 'package' it in a different way. Most professional financial planners, for instance, prefer to call it 'proper allocation of funds' to make their clients accept the idea of budgeting.

The true value of budgeting

When we follow a budgeting plan, we are not depriving ourselves. Rather, we are forgoing immediate gratification in exchange for greater rewards in the future. If you want to be successful in in the long run, you need to practice letting go of instant gratification.

We practice this principle consistently in all areas of life. Most people already have the budgeting skills they need. Most of us know how to avoid unnecessary expenses. If you commute to work for example, you may have selected a route that gets you to work with the least expenses. If we do not follow a budget, we would just take the most convenient means of transportation without thinking of the cost. Because we care about being efficient with our money however, we usually avoid expensive forms of transportation.

You are already practicing budgeting in most areas of your life. For most people, their budgeting progress is ruined by just a few financial activities. One of the most common areas where people lack discipline is in eating out. This is a big challenge for most millennials. Other people fail to budget well because of expensive tastes in clothing.

A person may be disciplined in the way he spends his money on food, utilities and groceries but when it comes to spending on things that make him happy, he loses control. If you want to reach your financial goals, you need to find out which financial activities hurt your budget.

By knowing about your spending weaknesses, you will be able to find strategies that will allow you to improve your budgeting performance in the future. You should practice budgeting every day. You should make budgeting a habit so that you will still practice it even when you are more financially stable. You should never stop budgeting.

Chapter 2: 7 Expenses That Are Destroying Your Budget

If all you are doing is squeaking by each month, you may have to re-prioritize your bills and expenses. There are certain expenses that you can't change. You need to pay your mortgage. You need to have a cell phone. You need to eat. However, you may be overpaying when it comes to these necessities – and especially your luxuries. Check out some of these unnecessary expenses to see if you can save a little by cutting back. You can use the extra money to pad your budget.

Your Travel Expenses

Buy taking public transportation instead of using your car every day can save you money on gas and maintenance expenses on your car. If you cycle or walk to work instead, you can even cut costs when it comes to gym memberships (or you can eliminate your gym membership all together this way). No parking tickets. No sitting in traffic. Staying in shape. Minimizing your carbon footprint. The good that comes from bicycling to work can do more than just save you money.

Exercise

Speaking of gym memberships. The average cost of a gym membership can be anywhere from $50 to $60 a month. That adds up quickly. You can work out at home and not spend a dime on exercise equipment. If you're not a fan of running laps in your neighborhood (I know that some neighborhoods just aren't that safe), you can save money by going to a neighborhood recreational center, buying a DVD fitness program, or utilizing a corporate wellness program instead of joining a gym.

Your Cable Bill

The average cable bills is slightly less than $100 a month. However, with the popularity of online streaming, paying a cable bill seems almost redundant. The cost of an online streaming service (for movies and TV) is only a fraction of a cable bill and if you pay for internet already anyway, you shouldn't have to pay that much to watch a handful of TV shows.

You can even find a number of TV shows on YouTube (virtually for free since you already pay for the internet). Did you know that most libraries carry DVD's as well?

If you want to go even further, eliminate the need for TV shows all together and pick up a book instead. It will help your brain develop even further (Yay! Smarts!) and it's cheap entertainment.

Your Food Expenses

Eating out will always cost you more money than cooking your own meals. Dining out in restaurants will cost you hundreds. Even choosing cheaper dining options (fast food) will cost you money in the long run (health bills). Cooking your own meals is both healthier and more cost effective.

When it comes to buying groceries, buying in bulk and sticking to a grocery list can really help to pare down your food budget.

Now something that I've always had issues with is caffeine. I used to go to a coffee stand every morning on the way to work on once on the way back. This started to add up quickly. At $10 a day or $60 a week (yes, I would stop by on the weekends sometimes), I began to start seeing the savings of brewing coffee at home, rather quickly. While it might be a larger out of pocket expense to buy a good coffee pot and various supplies (depending on what you like to drink), you'll start to see the savings over time.

Your Cell Phone Bill

A lot of cell phone companies will pressure you into signing an expensive two-year contract. If you shop around, you will find that other companies (or even your own cell phone company) offer low cost plans that have no long term contracts. You can save nearly $100 a month with these plans.

Your Energy Bill

Even if you lower your thermostat by one degree, you can start saving on your energy bill. If you lower your thermostat by three degrees, you can save about nine percent on your energy bill. During the summer, you can save on cooling costs by paying attention to how you use fans instead of an air conditioner. Buying black out curtains, closing your windows during certain times of the day (and opening them at night), and using fans instead of an air conditioner unit can save you hundreds of dollars a year.

Your Entertainment Costs

Movies are the first thing that come to mind. Going out to see a movie these days costs a fortune. If you go to the movies once a week, that can cost you upwards of

$100 a month. If you choose streaming services instead and pop your own popcorn at home (bulk food stores can get you a gigantic bag of kernels and some of that fancy popcorn salt for a few dollars), you'll find that you have tons of extra money at the end of the month.

The savings don't end there though. Reading instead of going out to see a movie can save you all of your money. There are free movie screenings at certain museums. Some museums have free exhibits as well (art, history, and other types depending on what you're into). Check out some of these other free or inexpensive ideas for entertainment:

Day hikes and picnics

Outdoor activities at parks (like football games with friends, bicycling, canoeing, and camping)

Block parties with your neighbors

Movie nights at your house (with friends)

Game nights at your house (making it a pot luck will cut down costs)

Meetups with hobbyists can be inexpensive depending on your hobby of choice (meetup.com is a great place to meet like-minded people)

Chapter 3: Accrual And Cash Concepts

One relatively technical thing we'll need to get a good grasp of when it comes to personal finance management is the concepts of accrual and cash method of recording financial transactions. Let's talk about the accrual method first.

Under the accrual method of recording financial transactions, income is recorded or recognized as they are earned, not when they are received. Expenses, on the other hand, are recorded as they are incurred, not when they are paid out. What does this mean in layman's terms?

Let's say you're an engineer and you earn a living as a private practitioner. After completing a project, you are now entitled to your pay as stated in your contract or agreement with your client. Under the accrual method, you already record the income now because you already earned it, i.e., you now have a valid legal claim to such money because you already completed the agreed upon service. So your income for this month would reflect the pay from this project.

Under the cash method however, you won't record it as income just yet because you haven't received the payment. If the client pays you next month, only then will you record it as income.

As for expenses, consider your monthly electric bill. When you receive your billing statement, it's usually payable on a certain date in the future. You're given a grace period from the time you're billed to the time you pay the amount. Under the accrual method, you already record it as an expense for the current period because you already have a valid legal obligation to pay the amount, even if it's in the future. Under the cash method however, you record it as an expense for the particular period wherein you actually pay for it.

So what's the big deal about the different methods? Income and expenses will be recorded either way so why do we need to be aware of both? The reason: liquidity.

Liqui-what? Liquidity refers to our ability to meet our financial obligations as they fall due. Personal finance is about liquidity because we need money, not claims to money, to pay for our needs and wants. Let me illustrate.

For simplicity's sake, let's assume you only have one source of income – consultancy services – and only one expense – apartment rental. Further, let's assume you earned $1,500 from being a company's consultant but the terms of conditions of that engagement state that you'll be paid on the 2nd Monday of the following month. The rental on your apartment, however, is due at the end of the current month. Even if your income is 2 times your monthly rental, it won't mean much if you don't get it on time in order to pay the rent.

The risk with using the accrual method for recording and planning is that it doesn't take into consideration the timing of receipt and spending of cash. Using the accrual method for the above-mentioned example, you may think you're doing well because income significantly exceeds expense for the month but it doesn't tell you that you don't have the money to pay for the expense during the period. The cash method of recording and planning allows you to minimize your liquidity risk or the risk that you won't be able to meet your financial obligations. You'll appreciate this concept better in Chapter 2 on cash flow management.

TIME VALUE OF MONEY

One of the cornerstones of personal finance management is the concept of the time value of money, which states that our money that's available now is worth more than the same amount in the future because of the opportunity to make it grow. To put it another way, we'd be better off receiving, say, $100 now instead of $100 a year from now because we have the opportunity to make the money grow between now and 12 months later. This is the reason for charging interest on borrowed money and earning money from investments, particularly from lending money. This concept is the foundation for investing as well as debts.

OVERVIEW

The rest of this book will be dedicated to helping you meet your current and future needs by teaching you how to manage your finances properly through cash flow management (including budgeting), debt management, saving and investing your savings well. I will explain these concepts to you in a simple and straightforward manner so that you'll be able to really grasp these key concepts and help you understand more advanced personal finance reading materials later on.

CASH FLOW MANAGEMENT

"The fact is that one of the earliest lessons I learned in business was that balance sheets and income statements are fiction. Cash flow is reality." – Chris Chocola

Money moves in 2 ways: into our accounts or wallets and away from them. These movements are called cash flows and when it comes to ensuring our current and future needs are met, this is the key that'll spell success or failure in terms of personal finance management.

Why is that so? Remember liquidity or the ability to meet financial obligations when they fall due? It's dependent on how much cash we have and that is dependent on how we manage our cash flows. When we allow more money to move away from us compared to what moves into our accounts and wallets, our liquidity is compromised.

INFLOWS, OUTFLOWS AND POSITIONS

Events that move cash into our accounts and wallets are called cash inflows while those that move cash out from our accounts and wallets are called cash outflows. Examples of cash inflows are salaries, cash gifts and cash prizes won. Examples of cash outflows include bills payment, donating to a charitable institution, buying clothes or giving tithes and offerings in church.

If our cash inflows exceed outflows during a certain period, we experience what is called a positive cash flow position. When cash outflows exceed cash inflows, we are in a negative cash flow position. When both are equal, we have a square or neutral position.

Neutral positions mean that we are only able to meet current needs and without any surplus or savings, we won't be able to set anything aside for future needs. It also increases our liquidity risk – the possibility that we won't be able to meet our financial obligations – because if something happens to us that'll negatively affect our cash inflows, we don't have any savings or buffer to cover cash outflows.

Negative cash positions obviously mean we aren't able to meet current needs at all. Aside from failing to meet our current needs, being in a consistent state of negative cash flows every month will bury us deep in bad debts, which we'll discuss further in Chapter 3. Suffice to say, this can become a downward spiral of increasing bad debts and eventually, bankruptcy.

The ideal cash position is a positive one, which means we're not just able to meet current needs but we're also able to put aside money to provide for future ones. Unfortunately, consistent positive cash flows aren't easy to do because human nature gravitates toward spending as much money as is available. Enjoying positive cash flows may require a great deal of discipline and consistency to achieve but it's well worth it.

MAXIMIZING CASH INFLOWS

To maximize cash inflows, we need to identify 2 sources: recurring and non-recurring. Recurring sources – those that regularly provide cash inflows – include your job, business, certain types of investments and for some people, allowances from parents or companies. These sources are crucial to meeting our current needs because they offer a great degree of stability and consistency. Because current needs are recurring, most of our cash inflows should also be from recurring sources.

Non-recurring sources include work bonuses that are contingent on our personal and the company's performance, cash gifts, proceeds of sales of personal assets and occasional side income. We shouldn't rely on these for current needs because as we said, stability and consistency is key to meeting such needs and these neither stable nor consistent. These are good for complementing recurring sources, especially for saving up and investing for future needs.

One key to maximizing cash inflows is by establishing as many sources of recurring income as possible, also known by a more technical term called diversification. Basically, we don't want to put all our eggs in one basket, just in case that basket falls. By having several sources of recurring cash inflows, we lower the risk for disrupted cash inflows.

Another key to maximizing cash inflows is to establish recurring sources that are passive. Passive recurring income sources are those that require minimal active involvement in order to generate cash. In other words, these are sources that you can pretty much leave alone to produce cash inflows. Because these sources don't require much of your time and attention, you can set up more recurring sources of cash inflows and thus maximize them. We'll talk more about passive sources of recurring income – also known as passive investments – in Chapter 5.

Chapter 4: Basic Mistakes To Avoid In Budgeting

In this chapter, we have highlighted the common mistakes that need to be avoided while budgeting. If you take care of these common mistakes, then you are ready to say hello to a sound budget plan.

Forgetting to write down your expenses

Since it is not possible to completely follow our budgets, the only way we can perfect the upcoming budgets is by analyzing the present one and look at the deviations. These deviations are usually the additional expenses that we incur. Make sure you write down all your expenses as and when you incur them. Even if you are not able to update your budget immediately, do it before the end of the day. Don't forget to note them down. So it is always based on experience and trial and error. You cannot perfect your budget from the get go. You need to understand that various subtle things that can impact your budget in a big way. Don't forget to make note of the smaller adjustments, as they will also contribute towards raising your budget substantially.

Not writing down purchases

When we review our budget, we are indirectly keeping a track on our money. This analysis sometimes highlights the unnecessary purchases we have made during the month. Out of shame, we might not note these expenses intentionally. The whole point of budgeting is to ensure that we identify the redundant expenses and cut down on them. If you fail to note them down, they will never get tracked and you will start wondering where such a big chunk of money went. So even if it is a guilty pleasure like buying a toy for your collection, it is important to include it in your budget. Basically, count in everything that you think is an expense towards reducing your monthly income. Nobody will look at your budget to judge you and so, it is best that you remain as honest with it as possible.

Budget busters

In simple words, these refer to those expenses that are over and above the budgeted amount. If the difference is negligible, then it is not a matter of concern. However, if the difference is vast, then either watch what you spend next time or make room for such differences in your budget. As was said before, these might be small things that you think will not impact your budget in a big way but in reality, they will actually turn out to be big numbers. So don't take any expense for granted and account for everything that there is to. You will not think spending $4 on coffee a day will amount to a big number but expenses are always cumulative and over a period of time, you will realize you have lost a lot of money that you cannot even trace back.

Being conservative

One of the biggest mistakes when it comes to budgeting is being frugal. When you draw up a very conservative budget, you will obviously end up spending more than what you expected to spend. Since a frugal budget does not take into consideration any extravagant expenses, you will obviously end up spending outside the budget. The outcome of having a frugal budget is that you will feel frustrated for not following it properly. So try and include everything that you think you will incur on a monthly basis. A sample budget has been attached at the end of this chapter in order for you to understand how it works. Everything that a person might incur has been added in and it is best that you use it as a template to follow. An emergency amount has not been added in because adding one might tempt you to use it up and exhaust it by the end of the month. So it is important that you not add one at all and even if you do, you add in just $10 as the budget.

Not considering the time value of money

Often when we prepare budgets for long term, we forget to take the time value of money into consideration. Hence our budgets will not be completely accurate. Time value of money simply means that the value of ten dollars today is not same as the value of ten dollars after one year, given the inflation rate. Always take into consideration the time value of money when you are preparing a long-term budget such as planning for your retirement. You need to bear in mind how things used on a daily basis will be spiked up and must plan according to how much you will need in a month. Retirement savings are discussed in detail further in this book.

Sample budget for your reference

Sample budget

Monthly Incomes		Monthly Expenses	
Monthly salary	$2000.00	Rent/Mortgage paid	$400.00
Passive	$500.0	Personal	$300.0

income through food sales	0	loans paid	0
Portfolio investment: interests and dividends	$500.00	Credit Card charges	$400.00
		Utilities charges	$100.00
		Healthcare/ Medicines charges	$40.00
		Gas/ Transportation charges	$100.00
		Food/Groceries bills	$160.00

		Singing Class fees	$60.00
		Personal Care expenses	$40.00
		Clothing expenses	$100.00
		Night out with friends	$300.00
Total Income	$3000.00	Total Payable	$2000.00
Total income	$3000.00		
(-) total expenses	$2000.00		
Surplus	$1000.00		

Remember that this is just an imaginary budget and yours might look different. You must prepare one that is true to your incomes and expenses. Don't leave out anything and if your expenses are surpassing your income then choose to adjust your budget and make the two match. If they are not matching then try and cut down on certain items like the singing class for a month or two until your finances stabilize. Once they do, you can rejoin these classes.

Chapter 5: Effective Budgeting Strategies For Greater Financial Control And More Savings

Besides having the compound effect work for you as early as possible, your ultimate goal is to spend less than you make. When you do this, it will help you to get out of debt, save for emergencies, and save for retirement.

Below are budgeting strategies that will help you have a tighter grip on your financials:

1: Comprehend the goal

The goal of having a budget in place is not to track every single penny. In truth, you could know where every single dime goes and still have messy finances and too much debt. Sure enough, knowing where all your money is going is one way to budget, but it really is not the goal.

The goal of any budget is to help you SPEND LESS THAN YOU EARN, and focus your spending so that you waste nothing.

2: Track your spending for a week straight

While we have made it clear that the ultimate goal is to ensure you spend less than you earn, tracking every spent dime for a week or two week will be a massive revelation.

Ideally, you should track your expenses for a month, but tracking for a week is a great place to start. By doing this, you will be able to discover any unnoticed or underrated areas of spending.

3: Use the three-category budget

Most of us do not really need to know where every dollar goes. For example, knowing the exact amount you spent on gasoline for the month of April may be interesting and all, but it does not necessarily mean you will change your behavior. There is little point in tracking such an expense.

Many of us tend to overspend on just a few select categories such as eating out, new clothes, gadgets, entertainment, etc. Using the data you will accumulate from tracking your spending for a week straight, select 3 budget categories you would like to have firmer control over. You will notice that all of a sudden, it is very easy to tame your spending.

4: Use a credit card for most of your buys

Many financial gurus will advise you to use cash when buying things. They are right: parting with cash leaves an emotional imprint that helps you spend clear-headedly. However, a credit card allows you to know exactly how much you spent; it allows you to have this information on your fingertips. When you use a credit card, you will have a clear idea of how much gets out and contrast it to how much comes in. The problem with credit cards is that it is often too easy to just whip the thing out and swipe it.

5: Save first

This is the absolute strategy, and the only reason it does not appear as the first tip in this chapter is because we have dedicated an entire chapter to it. The "pay yourself first chapter" alludes to this strategy. Before you do anything with your money, have an automated system that immediately transfers a certain amount of money to a savings fund.

The other thing you need to do is to supplement your income to increase how much you can invest to get the most from the power of compounding.

Chapter 6: Start Creating Your Budget

Know your spending history

In creating a budget plan, the first step is to track your spending history. You need to know how much money you spend every month. Start collecting your bills, receipts, and credit card statements in order to have an accurate estimation of your monthly expenses. Sum up all your expenses and revenues for the past few months to know your total expenses. By doing this, you will be able to know how to design your budget plan that will fit in your financial status.

Also, identify how you're spending money currently.

Choosing a budgeting material

Nowadays, there are a lot of personal finance software that can be used to help you budget. These programs have many features that help you design your budget, understand your spending habits, and help you project cash flow in the future. Some of the examples of these budgeting software are Microsoft money, BudgetPulse, AceMoney, Quicken and Mint.

If you choose not to use budgeting software, you can still design your own budget plan in a spreadsheet. You can choose Microsoft excel or you can download a free spreadsheet program as long as it is compatible with your computer. Using a spreadsheet in tracking your income and expenses will help you minimize mistakes and make calculations easier. It can keep a running total of your finances which automatically adjusts every time you enter a new expense data.

If you want a least-expensive option that doesn't require a computer or an additional software expense, you can choose to use a notebook to record your budget plan. However, using a notebook is quite dangerous because you might misplace it and pages can be tore or get wet. It's also difficult to track and record long-term expenses with a notebook.

Calculate your income

Make a list of your income sources such as self-employment income, wages, pensions, commissions, child maintenance, or other regular sources of income. If you are a freelancer or an independent contractor, estimate how much you're likely to earn in a month. Calculate your income and subtract your estimated taxes to arrive at a more accurate amount of money left.

If you are a regular and salaried employee, subtract automatically your monthly taxes.

Make a list of your expenditures

The next step is to make a list of all your monthly expenses. This includes the bills that you have to pay every month, the amount of money that you spend on groceries, transportation costs, utility bills, or the amount of money that goes to shopping and other stuff. It will help you have an accurate view of your spending habits and unnecessary expenses. Gather all your credit card statements, receipts, bills, or other spending information to have an exact record of your spending.

Identifying expenses is an important process because it will help you know your common mistakes in spending and helps you track unnecessary expenses. The main purpose of it is to find out where your money goes every month.

Start recording your expenses from the least to the bigger amounts. You can also categorize your expenses into fixed and optional. Fixed expenses include bills, food, loan debts, transportation expenses, and other necessary things such as household products and clothing. While optional expenses include entertainment, luxuries, vacation funds, and savings.

Set priorities

One of the most important processes in creating your budget is separating your needs from wants. In designing a budget, you should know how to set your priorities. As you track your spending, you will discover that some of your money is spent on things that you don't really need. When you don't make a clear list of the things that you need, you will most likely purchase things that you may not need or spend more than you've planned. You should cut back on impulse spending when you're starting on a budget.

The key to having an effective budget is to separate your needs from wants or setting a priority list. Know the things that you really need and make them your priorities. If you don't know how to distinguish your needs from wants, try not having some random things for a period of time. If you realize that you cannot really live without it, then it is a need.

Set your goals

After you have made a clear monitor about your finances, you are now able to determine how much money you have left every month. Decide what to do with that money and set goals to accomplish.

In setting your goals, you need to identify what is important to you. Write down the things you want to have or a financial status that you want to achieve. By doing it, you will have a strong motivation in maintaining your designed budget.

You can have short-term goals such as:

- Having a house for the family

- Help your family members attain an education

- Start a business

- Pay off credit cards

- Apply for a business loan

- Buy a new car

- Travel or have a vacation

- Buy a new appliance

While on the other hand, long-term goals may include retirement plans, help children start out on their own or live without financial worries. You can choose whatever is important to you and design your goals well. Most people overspend because they don't clearly know what they want to do with their money. That is why they often use it to buy unnecessary things and spend money randomly. Clear goals will help you build your plan and serve as targets to aim. By having it, you can easily map out how you will achieve them.

After setting your goals, plan how much you need to save every month and for how long are you going to do it. Think also of how to accomplish that savings. Your goals should be realistic. Start planning for your success!

Start designing your budget plan

After you have ensured that your expenses do not exceed your income, set your goals and have separated your needs from wants, you are now ready to design your budget. This is where you make a plan based on what you've learned from your spending information.

Organize your budget plan into categories such as incomes, necessary expenses, bills, and other expenditures depending on your situation. Calculate your expenses and make some adjustments in a way that you will still have enough money to save. Make a list of the things that you need to buy every month and calculate your bills in order to estimate the amount of money that will come out of your income. Make sure that your expenses are lesser than your income. Think of different ways on how to save money every month.

Design your budget in a way that you can easily understand and monitor your finances. You can also ask your friends for ideas on a budget plan, try different designs, and find which one fits you.

Chapter 7: Creating A Good Budget

Your purpose is not just to create a budget but to create a good one. You are more likely to achieve your goals if you have a good budget. So how do you make one?

Step 1: Define your why

Before you create your budget, it is important to know why you need a budget. Your aim should be to sort out your money priorities and find the balance between your spending and earning. This simple process could help you to successfully pay your debt, plan better for your bills and save up for a major purchase or even a fun holiday. You need to set realistic goals on what it is you want a budget to do for you. How would you want your finances to look like in a year's time? Once you know what's important, use this to develop your money goals. For example:

Don't be scared that this could be complicated because it really isn't. You could set a short-term goal of paying off a certain amount of your debt, purchase a new appliance, go to a certain destination etc. As you set these goals, ensure to follow the SMART acronym i.e. Specific, Measurable, Attainable, Realistic/Relevant and Time Bound. Having clear goals will make it easy to allocate resources towards such goals because you have already prioritized what's important to you. You can structure your goals in the following manner:

Tip: It is often more motivating to write down the figures on a piece of paper. As such, feel free to write down something similar.

Step 2: Tracking Your Day To Day Spending And Income

After getting a clear understanding of what your goals are as far as money goes, now is the time to know where the money goes. We have our unique habits when it comes to spending. Some of these habits could be positive while others could be the reason why we are always struggling with finances.

The small things that we spend our money on are the ones that end up adding to the high costs. Take note of the very small amounts of money that you spend each day. Get to know how much they add up to at the end of the day. You can do this by creating a spending diary, a small book that you note down every small amount of money that you spend to the last dollar. It is from here that you will get to know about your spending habits. This is what is referred to as tracking your spending. Start by choosing how long you want to track the spending; one week is usually the minimum time.

The same case applies to your income; note down every source of income that you have; it could be your business income, child tax benefits, commissions, wages etc. Whatever money you get on a regular basis, note it down. This could be pretty easy because in many instances, our sources of income are quite clear so there is no trouble about knowing how much you earn.

Note; Don't track what you think you should be spending. Instead, track what you are really spending and what you are really making.

So what do you use to track? Here are a few ideas:

Notebook and a Pen: This one is an old strategy but it works just fine. You can use it to track every item with ease. You can record each expense item category on its page so that you can have more space to add notes for each expense item. You can even print budgeting templates (like those in PDF) then fill out everything. Here is a completed monthly expense file to help you understand how this is done.

Spreadsheets

This is one of the simplest if you know a thing or two about computers. The good thing with this one is that you will get many downloadable templates out there so all you need to do is to fill out the respective entries nicely.

Financial Software

You can use Mint.com or any other software to track your expenses.

Finally, compare your income and expenses to know how much remains or the deficit. There will be times when your expenses exceed your income possibly because you received a tax refund, you incurred credit card debt and others. If you don't like how your money is just disappearing and are tired of having to postpone your financial goals, now is the time to take action to manage your money as opposed to money managing you.

Use the information you have from the expense tracker you've just been following to understand your spending behaviors then determine why you spend money on a certain item. I will highlight some of these behaviors then mention a thing or two about how to deal with them:

Buying name brands

Well, obviously, you might think that you are a loyal customer to a certain brand but have you considered buying generic or previously owned products? You might discover they are just as good. Don't let your biasness affect your spending.

Impulse buying

If you find yourself buying stuff you had not budgeted for, then you can instead set an allowance for yourself from where you can spend money on anything you want. Include this into your envelop system if you really want it to work. Also, try not to carry any extra money or credit cards when you go out looking for stuff. You might just end up buying things before thinking clearly about them.

You don't know where your money goes

Now you really know where your money goes. Keep tracking it.

Spending all the money without saving

You can fix this bad habit through saving through direct deposit.

Step 3: Identify The Priorities

Throughout the one or so month, you've simply been tracking your spending and expenditures. If you've understood how much you spend on every single item, you can start removing the items that you can live without. Obviously, there will be items that you've been spending on throughout the tracking period that you really shouldn't have been spending on. Define your needs and wants. Needs are the things you cannot live without like food, housing etc while wants are the things that you can live without. You have to categorize your expenses either as needs or wants. The idea here is to help you to know what you need to get rid of and what you should keep. You might discover you take too much coffee or spend money on other expenditure items too much hence the need to cut down on these.

Note: Budgeting is about being intentional with your spending and saving. Establish your needs and wants and learn to prioritize the two. Your wants are the desires that you have but can do away with. Those are the first things that you should do away with when you are thinking of cutting down your expenses. This is the part that you can learn how to save and later invest. Set the goals for your future and learn how to save for them. It is easier to work with a goal in mind. When planning your goals, get to know the short and long time ones. This is the crux of budgeting

Listed below is an example of each of the expenses but this might not apply to everyone; some people's needs may end up being the others wants.

Needs; housing, transportation, utility and groceries

Saving/ financial priorities; retirement contributions, debt payments, types of savings

Wants/Lifestyle choices; cable, internet entertainment, personal care, general shopping

Note:

The expense tracker excel sheet or the PDF file that you have been using is a good place to start when categorizing your expenses on whether they are needs or wants.

Obviously, a budget would be useless if you don't aim at cutting down on the unnecessary expenditure. If you don't cut down on your spending, everything will just be another monthly tracker. As such, you should start by cutting down on wants. But don't cut everything; you still need some money for fun otherwise you will give up altogether when things don't seem to be the same again. However, ensure that you budget for what you call fun.

After you cut down on wants, the next phase is figuring out how to save on your needs. One way of ensuring that you don't end up screwing up everything is having rigid rules on how much of your income you should spend on different expenditure categories.

To put this into perspective, let's discuss some budgeting rules that you can follow to make your life better.

Budgeting Rules

Rule #1: 25%

For starters, go through your expenditure schedule above then categorize each of the items into four parts such that all your expenses are categorized into 4 categories namely taxes, living expenses, debts (excluding your mortgage payments) and housing (mortgage and or rent).

Allocate the first 25% of your income to taxes

Well, obviously, you are taxed before you even receive your money. Do an estimate of how much money accounts to taxes. So between the different and federal assessments, set 25% of your pretax income to these.

Allocate the next 25% of your income to housing

It doesn't matter whether you own a house or rent; ensure you don't spend more than 25% of your pretax monthly income on housing. This means that your mortgage or rent payments shouldn't exceed more than a quarter of your income irrespective of how much money you earn.

Allocate another 25 percent of your pretax income on debt

Set a limit of 25% for all your loan payments. This excludes mortgage repayments. Just as a note, the closer your debt obligations get to 30% of your pretax income, the higher the likelihood that you will find a hard time accessing credit.

Finally, allocate 25% of your pretax income on living expenses

This is where you spend everything else. Your savings should be in there, food, groceries etc.

Tip: If you save on each expenditure category, you will obviously have something left on the side to save, invest and increase your emergency kitty. This is the only way you can stop living from paycheck to paycheck. For instance, ensure your emergency kitty has at least 3-6 months of your monthly living expenses.

Note: Ensure to track everything if you really want to succeed at it and in knowing your expenditure habits.

Rule #2: 50-30-20 Budgeting Rule

This is obviously the one rule that will help you to learn how to categorize your wants and needs. So how does it help in getting you to do that? Well, let's see how it works just to help you understand how it can actually get you to transform your life.

In this rule, you divide your after tax income i.e. net pay into 3 broad categories then apportion as follows:

Allocate 50% of your net income on needs/essentials

This includes anything you cannot live without or avoid at any given month. It includes such expenses like auto loans, mortgages, credit cards, rent, groceries etc. Broadly, this category should have expenses like housing, groceries, utilities and transportation.

Allocate 30% of your net income on wants or lifestyle choices

These are personal and voluntary expenses that you can probably forgo if you want to such as cable, charity giving, phone plan, gym fees, personal care, entertainment, shopping, restaurants, pets, childcare, internet, etc.

Tip: If you've taken care of the other categories of expenses, you have nothing to worry about. But you can cut down on this if you have the willpower. If an expenditure fits within your 30%, you are spending responsibly! Having a budget for this can keep you motivated knowing that you have an allowance to splurge.

Allocate 20% of your net income on debt and saving

This category is for helping you to pay up your outstanding debts as you also contribute towards a retirement fund, your emergency fund etc.

To help you understand this better, let me give you an illustration that will put this into perspective.

Meet John, who is in his first job and takes home $2,250. He has student loans to pay but he is able to manage that and contribute to a Roth IRA and pay his bills comfortably.

Annual income: $36000

Take Home After Taxes (we are assuming that taxes and 401k contributions take up to 25%: 2250

Needs/Essentials 49%

Transportation; $75

Housing; $750

Utilities; $75

Groceries; $200

Total: $1,100, which is 49% of net income

Debt and Saving 21%

Retirement contributions; $225

Emergency funds; $200

Car debt; $50

Total: $475, which accounts for 21% of net income

Lifestyle choices 30%

These totals up to 675, which accounts for 30% of net income

Obviously, your expenses will be different from the other person; what's important is to monitor your percentages just to make sure that you don't end up in financial distress. Actually, you can cut down on some areas and increase on others. For instance, you can reduce your lifestyle choices to 20% and increase your debt and savings allocation to 30%. Whatever works for you is ok. But the most important thing to remember is that your lifestyle choices should never exceed 30%. Anything else can go up and down but your lifestyle choices can only go down. You can survive without these wants if you really want to transform your life.

Note: As you will notice, your retirement contributions are not in the calculation since they are not part of your take home pay. This simply means that you are actually contributing more towards debt and savings than the breakdown actually suggests. However, leave this as is; your retirement money should never be part of your current calculations when it comes to budgeting. Out of sight, out of mind!

If you want to learn whether you are really following the 50-30-20 rule, you can use Learn Vest to help you do that with ease.

Chapter 8: Setting Goals

Right now your head is probably spinning. This is a lot to take in, but stick with it – it will serve you well.

Balance plus.

Subtract your expenses from your income. Ideally, your income should cover your expenses with some left over. However, many of us live outside of our means. So, your first goal is to make your income exceed your expenses. Once you get a handle on your money, make sure you budget a little money for entertainment to treat yourself for doing such a good job. Just don't overdo it.

How? Cut out those monthly pedicures. Stop buying your coffee at coffee houses. Get up 20 minutes earlier and make it at home. Stop taking cash from the ATM until you can better regulate how it is spent. You get the idea. There are likely at least two ways to trim fat from your budget right now - probably more.

Set up an Emergency Fund.

This is not for that sweater that finally went on sale at Macy's, or to pay your mortgage when you have overspent your budget. It's for true emergencies: the car breaks down and needs a $700.00 part that takes 3 minutes to put in, or you fall and break your leg and your deductible is $1500, that sort of thing.

When you overspend your budget, you can still find places that you can pull money out of to help you pay your mortgage this month. That's the beauty of a budget. You know exactly what you do and don't have.

Pay Down Debts

Your next goal should be to use the extra money you have either found in your budget, or created through hard work and sacrifice to pay down your debts. It is probably best, depending on the nature of your debts, to pay the least first. Then you get the satisfaction of checking them off of your list faster. Still, remember to leave a little something for yourself – you've worked hard to get here. As an added bonus, as you pay off those debts, you increase the available money in your budget.

Saving.

Once you've accomplished these, or at least you are well on your way, you will want to think about saving for other things. You could save for your children's college, your retirement, a new car, or even a vacation. All of this is possible through the power of the budget.

You know what's coming in each month, you know what's going out. Even if both fluctuate, you've taken that into account. You can now visualize your financial life and manipulate it to suit your needs.

It is important to treat "found money", like an unexpected dividend from your car insurance company, as any other income. Allocate it where you need it most. If you are good with outflow, then allocate it to one of your funds, like the emergency fund. Don't just go out and blow it.

Another great way to help you meet your goals is to allocate all of your annual raise to the funds you have set up: emergency, college, retirement etc.[6] You are already living within your means, so don't increase those means by spending more when you get that raise. Get it?

You can pretty much set any financial goal you want for yourself using your personal budget if you are honest with it and keep up with it properly. Which brings us to…

Avoiding Mistakes

The best way to avoid mistakes is to keep up with your budget on a daily basis. Here's an example. Let's say you are using Excel to do your budget. You've budgeted $67 for medical expenses because you know you will have to pay some co-pays this month. You go to the pharmacy and your Rx was for 3 months ($7.91), not the 1 month ($3) co-pay you budgeted for. When you get home, go straight to your budget and type over the co-pay you had on your list with the actual co-pay and Excel should refigure it for you. Now you know that you may have to shift the difference, ($4.91), from somewhere else to cover other items.

This may seem like a tiny thing, a trivial amount, but if you let several of these go, you could get into real trouble. The same is true with cash spending. There, you don't have the computer (if you have online banking) to show you your account daily. You have to rely on your own accounting. And if you write checks, you are in the same situation essentially because they take some time to post to your account. Each debit from your account must be accounted for in your budget. Make sure you allocate your cash and checks to descriptive categories, rather than just "cash". In other words, you want to say, "eating out" or "Starbucks's". Otherwise you won't know where the money is going.

Besides not having a budget at all, one of the biggest mistakes you can make is not having an emergency fund. You never know what might happen: car repairs, medical bills, broken glasses.

Another biggie is impulse spending and we're going to talk about that some more a little later. But, you've got to stick to your budget or it all falls apart.

The last mistake we're going to mention, and again, we will talk about this a little later, is spending your tax refund, raise, bonus, and dividend, whatever. That money should be thoughtfully put into your budget. You may need more money in your emergency fund, you might need to pay into savings, or pay down debt. You can still keep some for entertainment, of course, but you have to see the big picture. After all, isn't that why you did the budget in the first place?

And that's the key to a successful budget. You have to know where your money is going before you can harness its power. Once you know what is going on with your money, you can make it work for you, not against you.

Chapter 9: Popular Budgeting Strategies

The great thing about budgeting is that there are a variety of approaches you can use to come up with the budget. Owing to this, you choose a suitable budgeting strategy that suits your needs.

Let us look at some popular budgeting strategies and how to implement them:

50/20/30 Budget Rule

This method was popularized by Senator Elizabeth Warren in her book: All Your Worth: The Ultimate Lifetime Money Plan. This method is ideal if you prefer a hands-on approach to budgeting. 50-30-20's basic rule is to divide up all your earnings (after taxation) and allocate as follows:

50% on your needs (half of your after-tax salary)

30% on wants

20% to your savings

Let us highlight what expenditures fall under each of the above categories:

Needs

These are things that you need for survival, e.g., food and all bills that you MUST pay, such as rent and mortgage, health care, insurance, car payments, and utilities. In other words, these are the things you cannot do without, and you'll notice some items such as dining out, gym subscriptions, Netflix and HBO, etc. are not here.

If you have been spending more than half your salary on your basic needs, you will either have to cut back on your lifestyle, bring down some of your 'wants.' For instance, you can revert to a more modest vehicle or move to a smaller house. You should also consider having more home-cooked meals and using public transport or carpooling.

Wants

These are the things that aren't necessarily categorized as essential, but we love spending money on them because they make life more comfortable. They include ultra-high-speed internet connectivity, high tech electronic gadgets, vacations, tickets to sporting events, movies out, and dinner. There are definitely more that I have not mentioned.

This category includes the simple upgrade decisions you make and is the place you can cut costs on if you want to save more. For instance, instead of purchasing tickets to a sporting event, you can watch it live on the television. Rather than eating out, you can opt for home-cooked meals. You don't necessarily need to spend money on monthly gym subscription fees if you can workout at home. You can have a cheaper car if the one you have is very expensive to maintain.

As you do this, remember that budgeting is not about punishing yourself. If you love paying for that gym subscription and it is important to you, then continue paying for it, and you can look for other ways of cutting costs. If fine dining out is your thing, don't deny yourself that but find a balance.

Savings

Finally, you should allocate at least 20% of your net income for investment or savings. With the savings, you could invest in the stock exchange market, mutual fund, your retirement, coming up with your emergency fund etc.

Ensure that you always have no less than three months of emergency savings on standby in case of any emergencies. Once you have ticked that box, you are now free to focus on other financial goals you may be pursuing, such as saving for retirement or you could do them concurrently; save for investment as well as build an emergency fund.

Envelope Budget

Dave Ramsey started the envelope system, and it is a cash-based way of controlling your expenditure. With this system, you need to come up with an envelope for each category of your expenses, i.e. gas, groceries, savings, etc. Every time you receive your paycheck, you allocate different amounts of money into the various envelopes based on what you anticipate to spend in that category. Once you have used up all the money in a particular envelope, you will have to wait until you receive the next paycheck before you can spend again in that category. The aim here is to limit you to spend within what is available and prevent you from overspending.

To use this system, you will first have to list down all the categories and set spending limits for each category. Remember that the total amount for all categories combined should not exceed what you earn per month. To determine what categories you should include in your budget, consider all the places and things where you spend most of your money.

Now list down all the common expenditures you can think about. Here are a few examples: groceries, utilities, health, car maintenance and gas, household items, kid's items, pet care, entertainment, clothing, grooming, and dining out, among others. Also, remember to include other irregular expense categories such as gifts, etc. Ensure that you tailor your budget to reflect your personal situation. To determine what reasonable limit you ought to set for each category, look at your recent banking receipts or statements to have a general idea of your overall spending. You could also track your expenses for a month to have an idea of what you spend on what. Now label each envelope and use only one envelope per category. Also, write "monthly budgeted amount" beneath the name of the spending category.

If you receive income on a bimonthly or weekly basis, divide the total monthly amount for every category by the number of times you are paid every month and write the figure on the envelope as well. This will enable you to slide in the correct amount of money into the envelope from the total income you receive.

When you've earned your paycheck, divide the money accordingly, and put the respective allocated amount for every category into the designated envelope. Assuming that you make $1000 every month, your envelope budget could look something like this:

$400 to the rent envelope

$200 to your grocery envelope

$140 to the gas and maintenance envelope

$140 to the utility envelope

$60 to the clothing and personal care envelope

$60 to the savings envelope

When you want to pay a bill or visit the local store, make sure you pick money from the correct envelope. After you have spent all the money from one of the envelopes, DO NOT take from any other envelope to continue with your spending. If you do so, you'll not only be falling short for that category but also setting a bad precedent going forward. You will basically be falling back into the old bad habits of overspending.

However, if you notice that you have some money left over in an envelope at the end of the month, you can either transfer it to your emergency or savings fund or leave it there for the next month's expenditure. You could also apportion it to something else that always seems to exceed the set amount.

Pay Yourself First Budgeting Strategy

This method is most suited for you if you don't get excited or have difficulty in developing and adhering to a laborious, time-intensive, and strict budget, especially when it comes to tracking your actual spending against the budget.

Instead of building your budget around your expenses, this method will allow you to build your budget around saving for the future. Let's see how:

Start by simply noting down how much you earn per month. In this case, we will assume that your monthly income is $2,000 after taxes. Now write down all the savings goals you have set for every aspect of your life. For example:

$100 per month set aside for future home maintenance and repairs

$200 per month set aside for retirement account

$100 (or more) per month set aside to cater for my child's education

$100 per month set aside to buy a new car

$50 per month set aside for immediate and future car maintenance and repairs

$25 per month set aside for future health, auto and home co-pays and insurance deductibles, which I should consider using an emergency fund

$25 per month set aside to pay for an annual vacation.

All these will amount to $600 every month going into your family's and individual future. Now take away this $600 from your monthly net income of $2,000, and you will have $1,200 left. You now have the freedom to spend this money; however, you want. Pay your bills, eat dinner out, and get coffee every morning; the choice is yours. You don't have to worry over what category you should allocate a particular amount.

This method is arguably the easiest budgeting model because you won't have to spend hours pondering over what fraction of your money should go towards electricity vs. groceries vs. rent. All you have to do is pay yourself first to secure your future and then relax and spend the rest on all other immediate expenses.

This budget may feel anti-ethical when you compare it to other traditional budgeting strategies, but it has proven to be equally effective. The main objective of this budget is to ensure that you're actualizing your savings goals without allowing over-expenditures in other areas to eat up what you earn.

Zero Based Budgeting (ZBB)

With Zero-based budgeting, your expenses subtracted from your income equal to zero, which means that your total expenditure during the month should match your total earnings. Basically, Zero-based budgeting ensures that you are assigning every dollar you earn a job to do. This is important because sometimes if we don't assign money a task to do when you have extra, you will find yourself spending it poorly when you could have used the money wisely.

Let's put this into perspective to help you understand. Let's assume that you earn $1500 per month. Everything you choose to do with this money, whether it's investing, spending, giving, or saving, should add up to $1500. This way, you will be able to track where every hard-earned penny is going. You'll be setting yourself for a heart attack if you don't know where your money is going every month.

So how do you come up with a zero-based budget?

Compute your monthly income

However, you choose to do this, whether, with excel spreadsheets, mobile apps, or the traditional pen and paper is fine. Your income should include every penny you earn from the regular paychecks to side hustles to child support to residual income, dividend payments, small business income, and all other extra cash you rake in. Add up all those figures as they will make up your budget.

Note down all monthly expenses

Before the new month starts, plan, and write down every expense. Begin with the most basic and essential; those that you can't live without including food, shelter, utilities, and transport. Once you have the essential expenses covered, write down the rest, you may spend money on during the month. Remember that needs vary from one month to the other, which is why you need a new budget, one for every month.

Don't forget to include a miscellaneous category in your budget because unexpected things can knock at your door at any time. If all goes well and until the end of the month, you can use that money to service a loan or increase your savings.

Note down all seasonal expenses

At this stage, think through the calendar year. Anticipate all expenses that will come up so that you can plan and save now. You know that Thanksgiving happens in November every year. So don't wait until the end of October to act like Thanksgiving suddenly snuck up on you. If your calculations tell you that you'll need at least $500 for Thanksgiving, then split that by the number of months leading up to November. This also goes for all other seasonal expenses like birthdays, holidays, and anniversaries.

Also, think of other irregular seasonal expenses that are required. Make sure you plan for things such as insurance premiums, HOA dues, property taxes, and car tag renewal fees, among others. If you think ahead and plan for these, you won't feel the pressure of an expense that has unexpectedly blindsided you.

Deduct your earnings from all expenditure to equal zero

While you want this number to get to zero, it may take some practice to get there. In most cases, it may take up to three months before the numbers align. So don't get worried or shocked if your expenses and income don't cancel each other out immediately. It is only an indication that you need to push some of the numbers down and some others up.

Just identify where you need to allocate less money and trim accordingly.

If you're spending beyond your means, reduce some expenses so that your overall expenses and income equal to zero. There are many ways to reduce expenditure. You can carpool to work, make coffee rather than buying it, use discount apps or coupons, cutting the cable, etc.

Track your expenditure

Once the expenses and income have canceled each other out, keep track of how you spend money throughout the month. This is the only way you'll know whether your spending is in line with your plan. If you have been overspending, you'll be happy when you notice that you're now winning money every month.

Priority-Based (Value-Based) Budget

This last one is more of a philosophy than a budget, but it still involves spending and tracking. This kind of budget is a bit different from your typical budget because it relies on quite a bit of self-discovery and soul searching. Instead of worrying about how much or little money you have allocated per category, you simply base it on your values and shut everything else out. It is most suited to persons who have a higher level of income.

To begin with, you should write down what you will allow yourself to spend on based on what you value. For instance, if you value new experiences, you can write down traveling. If you're thrilled with cutting edge technology and gadgets, write that down. Based on the list you create, go on and allocate fractions of your disposable earning every month to what you value. You can allocate a little less money to the next item in line and so on.

The idea of doing this is so that you do not spend money on anything else that isn't on your list. For example, if having the latest electronic gadget is on your list and not entertainment and eating out at restaurants, you should ensure that you spend your money correctly to get that electronic gadget you want.

This budgeting method will suit you if you are much more disciplined and very aware of your spending and/or already frugal with money, as well as if you naturally enjoy saving. If you don't like the amount of time it takes to track how you spend money, then this method is recommended for you.

If you feel like you've been wasting money on things you don't need or want, then this is a great budgeting method for you. By listing down all what you truly value, then you start putting your money on things that bring you joy and spend money on things that make you happy.

Now that you know some budgeting strategies you can use to budget, are you ready to start budgeting? Remember that you can always tweak any of them to suit your needs. A budget should be flexible to serve its purpose. Let us now learn how you can get started with budgeting.

Chapter 10: Writing Your Financial Plan

Think of it in this way, all of your financial plans are simply your budget on boosters. You are not just making plans on what to do with your next pay slip, but your life on the whole. A financial plan simply considers all factors and requirements and accounts them into your goals.

The best bit isn't complicated at all – it's simply figuring out what you want to do and knowing when it is that you exactly want to do it. As with the saying, the planning of a lifetime begins with a simple step of sitting down to make the plan. The final completed picture comes in play when you know how and when you'll get to your goals.

There is no process that is set in stone to making your financial plan. Each person has a different one. Create it in as creative a way as possible as long as you get to do everything you want somewhere along your plan.

Establish a timeline:

Where do you see yourself in the next five years? In the next twenty or thirty years? Set your plan in a way that takes all these plans into consideration. Make sure you include the following criteria and information when you create your plan.

Know essential costs: These are all your existing billing with an additional 5% taken as inflation (just-in-case). Add, of course, your insurances.

Know the cost of luxury: These are the little indulgences that we like to splurge on, on the odd occasion. Know how much you'll need for the type of life style you want. Houses, cars, vacations, education, everything that you can possibly think of.

Plan a strategy for income: For the majority of people, this is simply adding in their salaries. However, know that this is not just the only means of income. Begin a side job, a business that will make you some extra money for a rainy day. Any hobby, freelance or even online jobs are additional options you can explore.

Plan for investments: Remember that investments are simply an essential to counteract inflation. Investment can be in any area – stocks and bonds, fixed assets, gold, mutual funds, collections etc. Remember to keep track of everything you're doing and don't ever, ever keep all your eggs in a single basket. That is one of the greatest pieces of advice that Warren Buffet, investment wizard always teaches. As you increase in age, you will find that financial security is absolutely important.

Include every income & expense: Remember to consider every single possibility, every source of income and expense. Whenever you're unsure, add the numbers on the slightly lower side for income and on the higher side for expenses – it's always prudent to overestimate and have savings, rather than underestimating and forgetting everything.

The Key to a Good Financial Plan

Unlike common thought, it doesn't take much to write a financial plant, however, you need to do so with a good bit of creativity and rationality. Be clear and concise in your assessment of your present situation, thinking out rationally. Be creative to know what is possible, and simply have the integrity and courage to follow through completely. Remember that what is written on paper doesn't necessarily mean that it will come to pass – it is all up to how you decide to follow up and live up to your goals. This is the hardest step, and a place where most people lose their footing.

Always remember that the whole point of the financial plan is always your goals. Always. However, some of us get so wound up with the financials that we forget the whole reason for planning. Don't forget, money is just the tool, it's never about the money, it's always about getting what you need out of life.

Eliminating Debt

Sadly for us, debt is a disease that takes us from being quite happy in our lives to nearly always taking control completely over our lives. The majority of us aren't even sure how we have ended up in this situation. Buying on credit, swiping our credit cards and doing everything with a tiny piece of plastic loaned to us from a bank seems to be the theme of the generation. However, remember it is easy to break from the throes of debt. Don't let it control you. Seize control over your life simply by refusing to get into any more debt. And follow the following steps to end the debt that you have!

1. End the cycle. Don't acquire any more debt. This is the most crucial stage in your life. Don't wait for the right moment, don't wait for tomorrow, simply start right now. Acknowledge that you have a problem first of all. Tackle the issue head on. Remember

that admitting that your debt is not anyone else's fault but yours is difficult, but this is crucial. Quit spending money that you haven't yet earned on thing you want right now. Remember, your wants are never always your needs.

2. Quit spending. When in debt, the first thing to do is to destroy any credit card that you have. They simply do not help, but compound your problem. Trust me, once you destroy them, you won't even miss them.

3. Spend money on the essentials. Again, your needs are not your wants. Necessary expenses like groceries, utilities etc are important. Cable TV, on the other hand, is NOT! Make adjustments by looking at your average monthly spend, and cut down on what is not needed at all. Eat out less frequently, like once every other week. Use coupons that you can find all over the internet whenever you plan on shopping. You'd be amazed at how much you can save.

4. Save up to a rainy day fund. Establish this as quickly as you can. It is essential that you have a little saved up for yourself before you being to pay your debts off. Have a savings account opened up for your emergency piggy-bank, and set up a standing order to transfer a bit of your pay check to move money to this account as soon as your pay hits your account.

Start off with something realistic - $1000 to start off with. And keep this for emergencies always. Keep it in an account that is not readily accessible, but can be used in case you need it in an emergency. Do not under any circumstance, link it to your debit card. Don't damage your efforts by handing yourself the keys to your financial security. Keep the savings in an account where you can access the funds online, but without a debit card or cheque. In case of emergencies, you can then access the money quickly, but won't be able to use it otherwise.

In case of an emergency, in case you don't have your little piggy bank, you can end up spending money put aside for your debt on the emergency. Having an emergency fund ensures that your debts are paid off on time and that the emergencies are taken care of.

Control your spending. It might be difficult to stick to the plan that you've made, so first put aside the money for the contingency or emergency fund. Then pay your debts off. Then turn to paying your bills.

Only then, remove differing amounts of money, and pack them into small envelopes. While this may seem a tad old fashioned, it is effective at letting you spend only on what you need, as once the envelope is empty, you have nothing else to worry about on spending. Continue reducing your non-essential spending so that you can follow your spending plans.

5. Following this, you should be able to put a stop to your spending. Put a debt snowball plan into place. Order your

current dues from the lowest to the highest amounts.

6. Put aside a certain amount you want to keep aside every month towards your dues. Put the minimum payment on all other debts except the one with the lowest amount.

7. Put aside every spare penny towards paying this debt off, and then continue with the next one on the list in the same manner. Do not reduce the amount that you have demarcated to pay your debts off. As you keep reducing costs, you will find that you are putting aside more and more. Look for ways and means you can cut down. Use a cheaper cell phone plan, check if you can trade your car in for a cheaper one that serves the same purpose.

Where ever you make the cut, add that difference to paying your debts off. Learn to work online, or part time and get an additional source of income. Sell some of the possessions that you don't need on eBay or other websites including Craigslist. Bring in that extra pennies to remove your debt as soon as possible.

Update your planning sheet every day, and ideally every pay day. As you see the amount of debt decrease, you will feel more and more free!

8. Don't forget to celebrate your little victories, every step of the way. Make this challenge an adventure that you will remember. You will find that it is amazing to stop unnecessary spending and to gain full on control of your finances.

Set challenges to find more and more frugal ways to save, find ways to have fun with zero cost!

Tips & Tricks:

One of the greatest tips your financial advisor will give you is this – Don't read financial advice for the heck of it. This simply is a waste of your time. Make sure that you find something that you can do within the next hour, and don't try to get off your seat until you figure it out.

Most of the tips in this book are aimed at making your future and preparing you for it. It's always about the long run, the big picture or whatever you want to call it, of your financial plan. Having said that, it does not mean that there are tips you can't work on right now. I've added a few tips that you can follow to ensure that you have a a comfortable journey through your financial plan!

Remember, the moment is now. Simply put, don't waste any more time getting it together. The only correct time to begin this process is in the here and now.

While these tips are not in the order of importance, each one of them will greatly increase your skills at financial planning and thus improve your financial situation. Sit down until you find one you like, and tick it off − it'll take you less than a minute!

Subscribe to Financial Newpapers and Magazines

Just because you don't have a career in finance or you're not a CEO/CFO/Investor does not mean you don't need to stay abreast of what's happening in the world of finance. If you're not really sure of what happens in the world of finance, you sure are making it difficult to get by.

Subscribe to the Economist or the Wall Street Journal; some of the best reading resources you can find on money. You get to know a lot about what's happening in business, in the world and in the realm of economy – all inclusive of sections on personal money management and finance too.

Begin writing a "Money" Blog:

Get into the habit of writing about your financial journey. This hardly takes a lot of time and you'll find that there's quite a few people in the world who have similar experiences as yourself.

The advantage to this is also that you not only have your finances and your financial goals out in the open, but also have a sense of accountability, and of course, you will find yourself enjoying that blog.

GET THAT SAVINGS ACCOUNT:

Think about it, this is one of the first things that you need to get. However, not many people have gotten about to doing that. In case you have money in a checking account and not savings, even if you aren't using that money, it is simply going to waste. A savings account gets you interest on the amount you have kept aside, and it can also double up as a piggy bank. Make it online, so that you can link it up to your current account and get saving!

Map out your financial plan:

If you don't have this plan, then effectively you are simply unaware of what you are doing or going to do. You'll never know if what you're doing, the effort that you're putting in is taking you in the right direction or not. Without planning, no amount of financial tips are going to help out.

It isn't complicated math, simply an understanding of how much you're getting, how much you spend and how much you want to spend.

Know what you want in life, and how you plan on getting it! It's that simple!

Chapter 11: Budgeting

Budgeting is one of the most basic acts of financial planning, and it's a great starting point. You don't have to think long term or figure out how to invest your money; all you have to do is keep track of what money you have coming in and how much of that you're spending. All of this information is already available to you – you know what your salary is and your expenses are all recorded on your credit card statements – so it's just a matter of putting that information into a form where you can easily digest it and see the big picture.

Some people are intimidated by the idea of building a budget, but it's really not hard at all. First, you just need to look at what you're spending now. To do that, we're going to have you create a simple budget spreadsheet and record all the things you spend money on every month – looking through the last few months' credit card statements is an easy way to do this. I've created a template with some sample data, which you can find at https://docs.google.com/spreadsheets/d/1O8St0RiqMHu6qbg7lPVMCBgjgEZGk5t-94K_4QXULGE/edit?usp=sharing.   I recommend that you go through that as part of this exercise and change the information there to reflect your own expenses.

First, we're going to start with the essentials – these are things that are consistent and necessary, like rent, bills and debt payments. Record the amount on the first tab in the spreadsheet, estimating towards the high end if it's something that isn't always the same, like groceries. Leave out anything non-mandatory like eating out and shopping.

Now that we've got the basics down, the next step is to record all of your monthly expenses that aren't mandatory on the second tab of the spreadsheet. Since these will tend to fluctuate, I recommend that you go through a few months' worth of credit card statements to get a feel for what your range of spending for each category is. When you record the amount, err on the high side – the goal here isn't to record what you'd like to be spending, but rather what you are spending now, and to that end it's better to be on the conservative side and estimate high.

Last but not least are annual recurring expenses, which you'll input on the third tab of the spreadsheet. It's easy to forget about these because they only come up once a year, but they need to be accounted for in your budgeting. These may include insurance bills that you pay yearly or your tax preparer's fees if you have your taxes done professionally. They also include things that aren't mandatory but reliably come up once a year, like travel and gift purchases for the holidays.

The final step is to input your income – that will allow us to find out how you stand financially right now. On the fourth tab, fill in the two lines for your monthly pay (this should be whatever you actually get in your paycheck after tax is taken out) as well as any other recurring monthly income that you receive from things like side jobs. If you do have side income that fluctuates, estimate towards the low end to be conservative.

Once you've filled out those two numbers, the spreadsheet will let you know how much money you have left over after your expenses, like this:

	A	B
1	Item	Amount
2	Monthly pay (after tax)	$4,321
3	Other monthly income (after tax)	$0
4	Recurring expenses	$2,027
5	Non-mandatory expenses	$1,075
6	Annual expenses (divided by 12)	$179
7	Remaining monthly cash	$1,040
8		

If you see a positive number, that's great! You're making more than you spend, which means you're on the right track. Still, there are a couple of additional things to consider:

Unexpected expenses – If your car breaks down or you have to go to the hospital, you're going to incur potentially large expenses that aren't tracked here. That's okay, since your budget is trying to make sure that you can save enough that when these do come up, you're prepared for them.

Saving – If you have a positive number but one that's very small, you probably still need to make adjustments to your spending. What's left is the amount you should be saving every month, and if that's only a few bucks, you're not going to make much progress or be prepared when unexpected expenses arise. Remember that the goal here is to start putting away as much money as possible early on, so that compounding can do its magic. Even if you have a significant amount remaining at the end of the month, it's still worth seeing if you can cut down your spending – never forget that because of compounding, every dollar you put away now is going to be worth a lot more in the long run than a dollar you put away next year.

On the other hand, if you see a negative number, it's time to make some changes. When you went through this spreadsheet, I advised you to be conservative with your numbers and record what you have been spending, not what you think you should be spending. Now's the time to go back through and see where you can make changes to your lifestyle to ensure that you have money left at the end of the month. That will mostly be in the second tab – your non-mandatory expenses. If you're in the red at the end of the month, it's time to cut down on some of that shopping and eating out. Adjust the numbers downward until you have a significant amount of cash left to save at the end of the month. If there isn't enough in your non-mandatory expenses to cut or you aren't willing to cut enough there, consider making lifestyle choices that will reduce the expenses in the first tab. Think about selling your car (I did this when I realized parking, insurance and gas were adding up to more than the cost of just taking an Uber everywhere I needed to go) or moving to an apartment that's smaller or in a cheaper location.

As you think about cutting expenses, remember that especially for those of you making debt payments every month, some of these cuts are temporary. Once you can save enough money to pay off a debt, that's going to be one expense that gets cut out of your budget, thus freeing up more cash. It's okay to spend some of this on yourself, as long as you don't go too far – when you get rid of a debt with a $200 monthly payment, consider putting $50 back into your monthly dining budget and saving the extra $150 (this is how you take advantage of the snowball effect I mentioned earlier).

If you don't want to cut expenses, or you just want to have even more cash left over at the end of the month to save, you can also look for ways to increase your income. These days, we live in a world in

which it's not hard to find a side hustle –
consider all of these companies that
employ people on demand on their own
hours:

Uber

Lyft

Postmates

Doordash

Caviar

Handy

Grubhub

The list goes on. I'll take this as an
opportunity to remind you of the power of
compounding interest. The best time to
earn more money is always today, because
it will have one more day to grow than
money that you earn tomorrow. Think
about this – if, for the next year, you drive
a few hours a week for Uber and make
$100 a week, which you put into savings,
you'll have $4800 by the end of the year. If

you put that away for the next 35 years and get a 7% return on it, you'll have over $55,000. There's no time like to present to increase your income, decrease your expenses and start saving!

Chapter 12: Cutting Costs

The next step in identifying various ways for you to cut your discretionary spending especially if you are adamant on maintaining your lifestyle. One way you can cut spending is to first start with your grocery spending.

If for example, you normally spend $500 on groceries per month then you can utilize websites that offer coupons so that you can still get the items you need for less. To get coupons you can get them from the manufacturer website, newspaper circulars, coupon websites and you also get coupons from the cashier at your normal grocery store when you check out.

A few years ago, couponing was a great way to get some items **FREE** or near free until television shows starting airing about thrifty individuals and as a result grocery store chains and product manufacturers stopped offering as many coupons for their products or no longer offered double or triple coupon opportunities so its somewhat harder but using coupons are still effective.

Keep in mind, grocery stores still have a 6 week cycle where they will change their product prices to their desired lowest amounts. You will need to time your coupons for these days.

For example, if cheese slices are let's say $3.99 for a 16 singles pack, and at their lowest they are $2.99, you will want to use your coupon then. The coupon may be for a dollar off. So instead of getting the cheese for $3.99 or $2.99 plus tax, with the coupon you will get it for $1.99. That is nearly 50% off. Keep in mind, the coupons typically offered enable you to get closer to 80% off.

There have been complaints at times where people have stated that they never offer coupons for products that they actually use or its never for stables like meat or vegetables and that's not entirely true.

As mentioned earlier, you will want to check coupon sites, newspaper circulars, magazines and the manufacturer website. Also at checkout, the stores usually give you coupons as well.

Following these tips will enable you to get the groceries you get anyway but at lower prices. When you start saving money on discretionary items such as groceries, put the money you saved and put it in your savings account. We will talk about savings in a later chapter.

With car fuel, you will want to utilize apps for your cell phone that help you identify the closest station with the lowest fuel prices and also utilize GPS apps that can help you identify ways to get home faster (time and distance wise) so you can save on fuel costs that you waste getting stuck in stop-and-go traffic. Yes you do waste gas in traffic more than roads and freeways where traffic flows at the same speed longer.

With other discretionary items such as cellphones, you will want to look at your phone patterns and if you have a habit of using less minutes on a regular basis, then maybe its time to lower your phone plan UNLESS you will lose major customer benefits switching plans, then don't do it.

When it comes to spending on eating out or spending on household items, especially if you do it on a regular basis, there are websites where you can get gift cards for major locations at a discount. If you search gift cards at a discount or similar keywords on any major search engine, you will come across websites where you can buy gift cards at a cheaper price. For example, you will have the opportunity to buy let's say a $25.00 gift card for $20 bucks.

Use these gift cards when spending on discretionary items that you buy on a regular basis. You will also want to utilize apps such as iBotta and Shopkick that will give you points or money you can redeem for cash or gift cards just for visiting, checking in and scanning products in places such as department stores, grocery stores, etc.

No matter what you do with any of the aforementioned tips, if you start to save money on a regular basis on things you normally buy such as car fuel, groceries, etc. Always make sure you put the money in your savings or you can do what we will talk about in the next chapter and split 50% into savings and 50% in paying off each debt as you go along.

Chapter 13: Making Adjustments In Planning Your Budget

Having a clear view of your expenses, income and financial goals, you are now ready to start planning your budget. If you are using specialized computer software, the program will automatically plot an ideal budget for you based on the financial data that you encoded. Using software will save you time and effort but you should understand that the program is not aware of your priorities in life. For example, it does not comprehend that you would like to spend less money on utilities and more on food for your family. Manually planning your budget gives you the total freedom to make personalized adjustments, so it is more recommended.

Step One: Plan Your Income

Creating your budget is a step-by-step process. Starting with your income enables you to know how much money you are going to be working with. This is an easier and a more practical approach to budget-making. Based on the previous financial data that you have recorded, determine your fixed income each month. Do not include your incentives and bonuses because these are variable and can change every month. Likewise, they are only additional income which you may or may not be able to earn. If your income is derived from business, it will be hard to come up with a fixed income each month because the amount depends on your sales performance. On a good month like December, the revenue from your business can double up but on slow months, your revenue can also suffer. In this situation, you need to use a conservative amount. This means, that the amount you are going to use as your income is the lowest revenue that you were able to generate. For example:

Revenue Made From Business

January – $4,000	July - $3,900
February - $3,800	August - $4,200
March - $4,200	September - $3,800
April - $5,500	October - $4,550
May - $5,200	November - $5,200
June - $4,100	December - $5,900

Based on this information, the lowest revenue generated was $3,800. This would be the amount that you would need to use as your fixed income. Now, write your fixed income down on the first part of your budget plan.

MONTHLY INCOME

Salary (Dad)	$4,500
Salary (Mom)	$4,200

TOTAL MONTHLY INCOME $8,700

Step Two: Plan Your Expenses

This is the part of your budget where you will be making the most adjustments. Now that you have determined how much money you make in a month, it is time to determine how much you want to spend monthly. Included in this part of your budget are your fixed and variable expenses, as well as your savings or the money required to achieve your financial goals. This time, you have to make sure that your total is equivalent to your total monthly income. You don't need to come up with a surplus because your savings are already included in the calculation.

If you are going to run short, try to make adjustments with your variable expenses. Typically, fixed expenses are neccessities and in cases of loans and mortgages, you have entered a contract that legally requires you to pay a particular amount each month. There's nothing much you can do about your fixed expenses but you can always minimize some of your variable expenses to come up with the money that you need.

MONTHLY INCOME

Salary (Dad)	$4,500
Salary (Mom)	$4,200
TOTAL MONTHLY INCOME	$8,700

MONTHLY EXPENSES

Long-term Goal	$1,000
Short-term Goal	$500
House Mortgage	$1,500
Car loan	$950
Insurance	$550
Utilities (Water, Electricity)	$800
Gas money	$900

Groceries	$1,200
Children's Needs	$700
Repairs & Other Household Expenses	$300
Emergency Fund	$300
TOTAL MONTHLY EXPENSES	$8,700

Double check all your calculations and feel free to adjust certain amounts as you go. As you plan your budget, be mindful of your priorities and remind yourself of the big difference between a want and a need. In order to achieve your financial goals, minimize spending on things that you can just do without. Now that you have finished creating your personalized budget plan, it's time to put it into application.

Chapter 14: Budgeting For Your Goals

Each financial goal is unique. You need to have a different approach in reaching each goal according to the amount that you need and the time left for saving.

Dealing with short-term financial goals

Among your listed financial commitments, you should classify each item whether they are short-term goals or long-term goals.

In budgeting, short-term refers to financial commitments that you need to pay within the next year. An example of a short-term financial responsibility is your bill payments. Some bills you pay every month. Let's say your electricity service company usually charges $100 per month. You just paid for last month's consumption. The next one will be due in one month. You have approximately sixty days to save for your next $100 payment.

If your salary arrives twice in a month, you have two chances to save for your electricity payment.

An immature budgeter will ignore it on the first payday and pay for the whole amount on the second payday. This puts a lot of mental stress on the budgeter when the payment date draws near.

A financially mature budgeter will set aside a fund for his electricity bill. He will save $100 dollars every month, $50 per payday. In times when the utility bill requires less than $100, he will save the leftover amount in his electricity fund. He will use this in the future when the electricity bill is higher than average.

You can deal with all your short-term payments in the same way. Here are the steps that you should follow when saving for short-term goals:

You should identify the amount that you need.

Then, you should check how much time you have for saving. You should then count the number of paydays you have between now and the goal deadline. If you receive other types of regular income, you should include them in the count.

You should then divide the total amount that you need by the number of paydays.

If you need $1000 in 8 months for example, you will have 16 paydays between now and the goal deadline. This is assuming that you are paid on a bi-monthly basis. If you use the method above, this means that you only need to save 63 dollars every month to be able to reach your goal. By doing it this way, saving becomes more manageable. Without this method, most people would only start saving when the deadline is near. As mentioned above, this creates a stressful experience.

Saving for long-term goals

Long-term financial goals are even more challenging. They are the financial commitments that you need to deal with more than a year from now. The challenge with long-term goals is that they usually require a big amount. Saving for a house for example, is a long-term goal. The big amounts required by these types of goals usually intimidate financially inexperienced people.

You should not allow the amount of money intimidate you. Long-term goals are challenging, but they can be achieved. To know how to save for your own long-term goal, here are the steps that you need to take:

Identify the thing or experience that you are saving for and the amount that you need. Knowing what you are working for will encourage you to work hard and save money. If you really want something, you will be able to mentally justify the sacrifices that you need to make.

Learn how other people have reached similar goals. If you are saving for a house for example, you need to learn the details of building the house in your area. You need to consider where you will get the necessary resources and work force to build your dream home. You should also learn about the financial solution services available for your goal.

In the case of building a house, you need to learn the types of housing loans available to you. Paying with cash is always the cheapest option. If you have a place to live in right now, you may choose to save money for your home to avoid the high interest payments of housing loans.

The best way to learn about all this is from people who have achieved similar goals. You should check your contacts for people who recently built or purchased a house. You should then contact them to get the information that you need. It is best to prepare your questions ahead of time so that you do not miss anything.

Identify the cheapest payment option for you

In our example above, you will be able to save for a house if you give yourself enough time to save and you can avoid high rent payments. For some people however, taking a housing loan is a lot cheaper if they take into consideration the amount that they need to pay for rent on the years that they are saving.

You need to consider all options on how to achieve your long-term goals. You need to study the ways that other people have reached their goals. After you have seen how other people reached similar goals, you should choose the cheapest method available to you without sacrificing quality.

Save slowly but surely

Just like with short-term goals, you need to save for your long-term goal every payday. Because you are saving for a big amount, you should save as much money as you can on each payday using the budgeting methods in the previous chapters.

Make your fund difficult to access

Because it takes a long time to reach your goal, you may be tempted to take out the money and use it for something else. To avoid this, you need to put the money in types of financial accounts that are difficult to access.

For goals that need to be achieved in the next two years for example, you may put the money in a bank account with no ATM card. To take out the money, you will need to go to the bank and ask for it from the teller.

Invest your money in your biggest goals

Some of the biggest goals require 7-20 years to reach. Saving for the kid's college fund, for example, takes a very long time. It is not wise to just let these types of funds sit around. You need to invest these types of funds in low-risk investment vehicles. This will allow the money to catch up with inflation in the saving period. With the amount of time spent invested, the money will be able to grow over the years and you may be able to reach your goals faster.

Chapter 15: Determine Your Yearly Expenses

Your yearly expenses are different from your monthly expenses. You have to spend money few times a year for many reasons; special occasions, holidays, property taxes, etc. There are type of expenses that we tend to forget when we make a budget, but they are what makes a difference! If you remember to include them, your budget has a better success rate!

What are yearly possible expenses?

Yearly possible expenses are situations, services or events that doesn't occur often and you have to spend money on them. You can't neglect them since they are necessary, so let's make them part of your budget. This can represent thousands of dollar, be sure to fill it.

What are holidays and birthdays expenses?

Remember Mother's day? How about Christmas? There's ton of holidays through the year along with birthdays of your family members. Know how much you will spend on each occasion so you can an efficient budget. Try to be rational with each events, since it's easy to feel emotional for each one of them. Preparing in advance will help when the time comes.

In order to determine your yearly expenses, I recommend that you open the **"Yearly Possible Expenses Worksheet"**. Follow these steps. Here's how you will do it:

Gather all your bills that fits the categories listed. Since all your bills are out, classify which ones are yearly expenses. If you don't spend monthly on a bill, it's a yearly bill.

Enter the expenses amounts in the worksheet. Under each category, enter the total of your bills in their category. If you have others yearly expenses that are not listed, calculate the total of them and add them in the Other section.

Enter the cost and the frequency for each category.

Divide by 12 the total. This is to find the monthly value of these yearly expenses.

Repeat the process for the "Gift And Holidays Expenses Worksheet".

Fill these data in your "Monthly Income & Expenses Worksheet".

What does it mean to entrepreneurs?

To an entrepreneur, it means to calculate all yearly expenses in your business. Everywhere where you spend money on that doesn't happen on a monthly basis. Find these amounts and follow these steps to find the monthly value of them, it will definitely help for a strong budget!

The Importance of Tracking

Tracking your budget means to keep track of your budget by watching your receipts, bills, etc., on a regular basis to know if you're respecting your budget. The best way to know if you overspend somewhere is to keep track of your spending. It's an important step of your budget since you correct your mistake or disciple your behaviors.

Why should you track your budget?

You should track your budget so you can achieve what you plan. If you don't take time to know if you respected it, what's the point of having a budget? It also helps you to rectify or adjust your budget. Your grocery budget was too small? Increase it a bit, but you have to decrease the same amount somewhere.

PS: I recommend tracking your budget over a period of time that you set for yourself, based on how busy you are and your level of commitment. I like to do it every 2-3 days so there's no overload. It becomes a habit. With once a week, you end up with too much paperwork.

In order to track your budget, here's how you will do it:

Duplicate each worksheet for tracking purposes. Have 12 of them. In each one of them, put the real amount you spent this month for each category.

Compare your new monthly worksheet with your initial one. How different is it? If you see that you spent less than expected, save that money. If on the same category you spend less for months, decrease its budget. If you overspend for months, increase its budget.

Track your savings. For your my

 saving, I setup a worksheet called "Goals Saving's Record". Use it to track if you're saving as much as you said you would.

Analyze your feeling. Have you did what you said you would? Where you able to resist the urge to spend more that you allowed yourself to? Are you comfortable with where you spent your money this month? If not, be more discipline with yourself.

What does it mean to entrepreneurs?

To an entrepreneur, it means to do your weekly/monthly/yearly balance sheets. They are important to know if you have or lacking money, along with if you overspent in what you wasn't supposed to. Control where your revenue goes is an important key in business.

Chapter 16: Effective Debt Management

Debt is one of the biggest clogs in the wheels of investing and savings.

Many people wish to start saving and investing but they find themselves caught up in so much debt that it becomes almost impossible to set aside anything at the end of the month.

The solution to this lies with developing a budget and repayment pattern that can handle your regular savings as well as your monthly repayments.

Here are a few steps to follow in order effectively manage and repay your debts while still committing your savings and investment plan.

Know how much you owe: First, you must make a list of your creditors and get a full picture of whom and what you owe.

Stop Incurring Further Debts: At this point, you have to stop incurring any further debts. Manage what you earn and let it be sufficient for you. Stay away from things you cannot afford except of course, it's a matter of life and death. In short, only borrow or incur debts if it's a health emergency. Any other thing can wait.

Tip: You can minimize how much you are exposed to risk related to health complications by taking a health insurance cover or setting aside an emergency kitty that would cushion you when you are in financial difficulty.

Create a Bill Payment Calendar: Late payments attract interests which could eventually add more to your debts so you should come up with a bill payment calendar that allows you to remember when bills are due so that you can pay them early.

Decide on Which Debts to Pay Off First: You should start with paying off your credit card debts because of the high interest rates. Pay off debts with high interests first before moving on to pay other low-interest bills.

Commit 20% of Your Income To Bill Repayment: Start using 20% of your monthly income to settle all your debts until you have cleared it out completely.

Chapter 17: Strapping Rockets To Your Savings

Now you have some savings that you built up through hard work and planning. What you need to do now is to make sure that you start to make those savings "work harder", and work for you. The ultimate objectives of proper financial planning are to ensure that you're able to save for, secure your future, and make you, "debt free." The combination of those two conditions is "financial independence". Here is how you attain it.

First things first

Here are two things that you should focus on, even before you think about investing the first penny of those hard-earned savings.

1. Take advantage of a 4o1(k) or 403(b) savings plan offered by your employer. 4o1(k) plans are retirement programs offered by private companies, while 403(b)

plans are offered by government institutions. This is an additional form of "forced saving", that is, thankfully administered by somebody else (your employer). The best feature of this plan is that the amount of the forced savings is deducted from your salary on a tax-deferred basis. What this scary term really means is that the amount taken from your salary is not taxed until you withdraw it at least until retirement age (59 and a half, or 65, the usual allowable ages). So your salary isn't taxed until after your contribution is deducted. This is worth an example:

If you make $3,000 a month, the taxable amount without any 4o1(k) or 403(b) deduction is the entire $3,000. For simplicity's sake, if your tax rate is 15%, you give Uncle Sam (i.e. the Internal Revenue Service) $450 a month plus whatever state taxes you need to pay. A 401(k) or 403(b) plan reduces that tax bill, and then some. For example, if your company sponsors a 401(k) or 403(b) plan, and allows 10% of your pay to be deducted from, and contributed to the plan, $300 is "saved" in the company plan as additional savings for you. Your taxable income now falls to $2,700 ($3,000 less the $300 contribution), and your monthly tax bill to the IRS goes down to $405 from $450. The tax on the $300 has been "deferred" at least until you reach 65. That's an additional $540 a year in savings.

But the benefits of a 401(k) or 403(b) plan don't end there. Most companies will even match your contribution up to 100% of your contribution! This is nothing short of a gift for you. No strings attached. It gets added to your contributions to build up towards your retirement fund. It only gets better.

You are able to take cheap loans from the plan for interest rates that are substantially below any bank or credit card loan. While you shouldn't even consider doing this, it is good to know that there are some funds available to you in case of an emergency.

A 401(k) or 403(b) plan also helps educate you about the nature of investments. Most companies will allow you to select what kind of investments you want your 401(k) or 403(b) nest egg to go to. You can invest from a range of funds classified as conservative to aggressive, giving you a useful introduction to money market funds, bonds, and stocks. Check with your employer on the conditions and limitations of their 401(k) or 403(b) plan if you are not already a participant. If you are, maximize your contributions as much as possible.

2. Try to reduce your existing credit card debt. Depending on the interest rates on your credit card, setting aside money to pay off credit card balances can have the same effect as saving money. If you pay only the minimum balances on your credit card, it can take you up to forty years to pay off the entire balance. You end up paying interest several times the amount of your original charge. That $300 cell phone may cost you $3,000 after you

figure in all the interest. Remember, too, that you can sometimes negotiate with your credit card bank to reduce your interest rates in exchange for lowering your limits and/or increasing your minimum payments. The object is to reduce your credit card as an emergency facility, not a means to purchase a lifestyle beyond your means. Credit card interest is an unneeded consumer expense. You can at least deduct mortgage interest from your income tax due. This used to be the case for credit card interest, but not anymore!

3. Set aside part of your savings for an "emergency fund". Many financial advisors recommend that you set aside three months' worth of income for any emergencies, such as loss of your job or medical emergencies. This will eliminate the need to use your credit card for your living expenses, and reduce the likelihood that you will need to use your credit card for very expensive cash advances as well.

Investing your savings

The last thing you want to do is to put the money you save under a mattress, or leave it in a savings account at your bank. With the average savings account paying less than 1% interest per year, you are actually losing money because inflation swallows up that 1% fast.

Investing in the U.S. market sometimes seems daunting and complicated. It can be, but it really isn't. Remember, however, that if you are starting you are a neophyte in investing, don't go all cavalier and put it all in some index or options fund that some online huckster tricks you into getting. That's like going to the racetrack and putting all your money on a horse you've never seen, or never heard of.

If you are afraid to start investing on your own, look for a reputable "investment advisor" that will allow you to invest at lower initial amounts. Be careful in these cases, because the advisor may steer you to securities or funds that he or she sells exclusively, maybe even being an employee of the fund. For me, the best place to start is at your bank or credit union. Not only do you already have a cordial relationship with them (meaning better access to advice), they probably have smaller initial requirements for investments.

For the more adventurous, I do not recommend investing in buying stocks or bonds of single entities; at least not at the beginning. Sure, Apple and Google shares look to be solid picks, but for a beginning investor with limited funds, you will end up with a few shares of a company, at best. Your financial life is then subject to the ups and downs of those companies. I strongly suggest that you invest in mutual funds first. A mutual fund is a fund pool comprised of funds from several investors who invest in securities such as money market funds, bonds, stocks, and others. Experienced money managers, whose goal is to maximize the return of those funds, operate them. You can invest in the "shares" of the funds for as low as $100, after a small initial investment, usually between $500 and $3,000. A mutual fund share sometimes represents a partial investment in dozens, even hundreds of companies, spreading the risk around.

You can also invest in options and index funds, which are essentially like mutual funds, but its pool of securities is more narrowly defined.

Dollar cost averaging

Regardless of what type of fund you invest in, the safest technique available to you is dollar cost averaging, which means buying the same amount of the same fund or security every month. For someone investing for the long-term, this lessens the risks of investing a single large sum in a single investment at the wrong time, like putting all your money in Yahoo! Stock when it fell from $400 per share to $50 in a matter of months. This method removes the stress of figuring out what is happening to an investment over time.

Individual Retirement Accounts or IRA's

Some investors may want to supplement whatever 401(k) or 403(b) plan they have. They may have excess savings they can put into retirement or are older people who need to supplement their retirement savings. These are "self-directed" plans, meaning that you need to find the investment vehicle yourself, and tax deferred. There are restrictions on early withdrawal and the penalties are pretty significant.

Long-term Care Insurance (LTC)

Some people are concerned about health care costs when they get old and do not want their children or relatives to worry about these costs when the need arises. Policies for these can be bought many years before the need for the care arises, and covers such costs as assisted living care, adult day care, nursing home, and home health care, especially for elderly people with disabilities, or those that require round-the-clock medical attention. These policies are usually very expensive, but they do provide some peace of mind.

Chapter 18: Paying Down Debt

There are no shortcuts when it comes to getting out of debt

~ Dave Ramsey

The first step in paying back what you owe is to get a clear picture of what you owe, and to whom. You'll need to list all your debts, the minimum payments and the interest rates on another sheet of paper.

While you are building your emergency fund, make sure you meet every minimum payment on time to avoid late fees. Once your emergency fund is full, you are going to start paying down your debt, starting with the smallest one, while maintaining minimum payments on all the rest of your debts.

Once the first debt is paid off, you will take the payments you were making on it and add it to your minimum payment of your next smallest debt.

If you have several debts that are approximately the same amount, you should pay the debt with the highest interest rate first.

Once the second debt is paid off, you will take that payment and apply it to the next debt, and so on, until your debts are paid off. You will be paying off your larger debts with larger monthly payments and by the time you are paying off your last debt the process will be accelerated because you will be able to make large monthly payments.

It sounds easy, and theoretically it is. The problem is when you are tempted to buy something you do not need. Don't be tempted to dip into your emergency fund or to pull out a credit card to pay for something that doesn't support your long term financial goals. If you still want the item once your debt is paid off, then you can buy it, as long as you don't pull out a credit card.

Another thing to consider is to put any "extra" money you get toward your debt. If you got an end of year bonus, use it to pay down some debt. If you got money for your birthday, treat yourself to less debt instead of dinner out. Rather than take a vacation with your tax return, pay off debt. You'll be amazed how quickly small payments can add up.

Create a chart, whether on paper or on a computer, of how much you owe and update it regularly. Congratulate yourself on a job well done when you reach a milestone, whether it be another $100 of debt eliminated, or a credit card fully paid off or anything else that is an accomplishment for you. Watching your debt shrink and telling yourself that you're doing a good job (no matter how silly that may seem to you) will help motivate you to continue pursuing your financial goals.

Debt Settlement Vs. Debt Management

Since it is true that 2.2 million Americans are facing debt, you can see many organizations working on these issues. You'll see both scams and legitimate companies offering advice. Most companies offer a free online or offline consultation. That should give you a good idea about their knowledge & advice. Overall, companies take information from you. A finance expert will analyze your situation, and a budget will be created. Next, the expert will talk to you regarding creditors, interest rate, taxes, and payments. He will guide you to pay the outstanding dues. These sessions give you confidence. Being in debt feels like a crime, but it is not. Hundreds of thousands of people have faced the same situation, and you are not alone!

How do you differentiate among legitimate organizations and scams? Here are the services listed by a legitimate company:

· Reduce your payments.

· Calculate & reduce the outstanding dues.

· Eliminate late fee charges (interest at the interest rate)

· Education about debt, credit card, money management, and budgeting.

Debt management companies exist to help you repay the outstanding dues. The banking system created these companies back in the 1980s. Their aim is to help consumers pay the debt. Debt management companies also help with the credit card interest rate. With a little bit of help, you can significantly reduce your credit card interest rate.

Debt settlement companies operate in a different way. Debt settlement companies ask you to stop paying the dues for about six months. The company will negotiate with the creditors to reduce the outstanding amount. If they fail to negotiate, they will offer you a little money when they have chunked out a big portion of fees from your pocket.

When working with debt management companies, they negotiate the matter with creditors. More often they close your credit card that simply reduces the interest rate. You will agree to pay a single amount. You will pay that amount, and you are free from credit card debt. Working with debt management companies do not have any negative effect on your credit score.

What happens when you refuse to pay credit card bills for six months? You will lose credit score points every month. As a good rule, you lose 50 points on every late point. It simply destroys your credit card score.

Next issue is cost. Debt settlement and debt management firms are two popular options. The cost of their operation is different. Debt management firms charge a monthly fee (25$). In addition to that, they either ask you for a flat fee (1,000$ or more) or a percentage fee that it typically 15%-20% of your debt amount. The cost of both options depends on how much the company can save for you.

Compare this to debt settlement companies who will charge (1500$-2,000$) with monthly fees of (20-100).

If you have compared carefully, the right option is the debt management company. A reputable debt management company can save you much more as compared to the debt settlement company. There are no taxes associated with the debt management companies. However, you'll pay the tax on the amount of money you saved. Let's suppose, you save 7,000$ then you will pay 1750$ as the tax. That should not be a problem since you have saved 7,000$.

Historical examples of bankruptcy and debt management

I am writing this chapter to give you some hope. It is a just an acknowledgment to let you know that you are not alone in this journey.

. Actor Nicolas Cage

You know that person? According to Forbes.com, the actor was worth more than 40$ million in 2009. That made him one of the Hollywood's most highly paid actors. Still, the luck does not favor you in every life segment. Nicolas Cage has faced serious financial issues. He sued his money manager reporting that he faced fraud. The manager told us a different story that indicated the actor had serious over-spending issues.

. Brendan Eraser

Known for the film, "journey to the center of the earth", Brendan had a smooth career until his separation from his wife. According to public records, his monthly earning was $205,000, but his expenditures were putting him in a debt of $87,000 every month.

. Kim Basinger

It is a famous story. In 1989, Kim Basinger bought the entire land of Braselton, Ga for

$20 million. The goal was to turn the place into a tourist attraction. Luck did not favor her as she was sued by main line pictures. She had to file bankruptcy in 1993.

. Lindsay Lohan

Lindsay Lohan faced serious financial issues many times. Add to that, she has problems with addictions. In 2013, she filmed some in-depth interviews with Oprah Winfrey that resulted in a $2 million dollar payout. Hopefully, she'll use this money to pay her outstanding debts and to enjoy the lifestyle she wants.

. Michael Jackson

Now, that is a hard story to tell. When Michael Jackson died, he was in a debt of 500 million dollars. His estate has generated over 750 million dollars, but still the estate executives are unable to pay all the dues. There are rumors that his estate will soon be opened for sale.

You have to be good at money making, but you must be damn good at saving money.

Money is a tool. Use it wisely and the world will bow before you. We say that material things do not matter for the heart relationships. It is like probably, we do not know how it feels when you owe 12,000$ to creditors. Enough of history and information, let's move to the real part.

Chapter 19: Budgeting For Credit Card Debt And The Envelope System

Credit card debt can cause a lot of stress and strain. The weight and worry caused by debt can lead to all sorts of problems. It can erode our ability to maintain good mental health. And when our mental health suffers, we lose self-control and spend more, creating a vicious cycle (Fay, 2018). So debt is painful and self-sustaining. Getting rid of it is one of the best ways to achieve health and happiness. Here are a few strategies that can help. The strategies shared here are valuable for those battling debt and for those who want to avoid debt.

The first thing you should do is to get rid of high-interest credit cards and replace them with balance-transfer credit cards with a 0% annual rate. This will minimize your cost tremendously. You should also make a habit of using the extra money to make an extra payment towards your debt. You should be aggressive in this regard, it does not matter how little the extra money is. Doing this will reduce your credit costs.

Another powerful strategy you can use is the envelope system. You pinpoint spending areas where you're consistently overspending. These areas can be entertainment, groceries, restaurants, and gaming. Just make sure that you group these areas into categories that make sense to you. Once you have done this, look at your income and start thinking about what would be the realistic and appropriate amount to spend in each category. Then get yourself some envelopes, and write down one category on each envelope. Withdraw cash from your bank and put the money for each category into its envelope. For instance, $300 for groceries goes into the grocery envelope, $100 on restaurants goes into the restaurant envelope, $50 on entertainment goes into the entertainment envelope, and so on.

Whenever you need to buy groceries or go for drinks or go to the movies, you take the money out of the corresponding envelope. When the money in that envelope runs out, that is it. You have met your budget for the month and cannot spend more on that category.

To make the most of this system, you should pick areas you have the most trouble with. When you need to go buy something, to avoid spending money on something you never planned on buying, take the exact amount you will need with you. So if you know that the grocery items you are going to get will cost you $100, then only take that much out of your envelope. To do that, you will have to make a shopping list and follow the list. If there is an item that tempts you, you will get it on the next trip. This protects you from making unnecessary purchases you might regret later.

Why follow the envelope method? For one thing, you avoid overdraft fees and overspending. It forces you to think every time you take money out of your envelope. You will make fewer spontaneous purchases. It also turns saving and paying off debts into a game. I mean that in the best possible way, games are motivating, they're fun and make us more creative. You will be faced with a challenge to keep within your limits, and the feelings of accomplishment you get when you do is worth it. The leftover money can be added to your debt payments.

The envelope system is attractive because it is easy to make and to follow. It takes away the surprise from your spending. No longer will you log into your account after a night out nervous about the balance, and then finding it lower than you expected. You won't have to think about how you will spend the remaining balance because all your money is accounted for. It can be mentally taxing to continually go over your balance and pending expenses whenever you buy something. This way, the mental labor is taken from you; the burden is lifted.

When we use cash to spend, we become more mindful and think twice about every purchase we make. The emotional attachment we make with tangible things is one of the factors that is taking place. We already form emotional connections with things we own that exist in our physical space. Because cash is already valuable and useful, it is much easier for our brains to feel attached. This means when we shop, we are likely to consider the costs. Card payments are much easier to make, and customers who use them don't think as deeply about the costs; to be frugal with cards one has to put in extra measures. The fact that people get incentives to use their cards—with things like rewards—can make it difficult for people to think carefully before they spend (Hamilton, 2017).

Chapter 20: Seeking Help From Professionals

Budget or credit counseling allows you to take control of your finances with the help of a professional budget or credit counsellor.

Anyone can get budget or credit counseling advice. These professionals will assist you in creating a realistic plan for managing your money, and help figure out other options that maybe budgeting alone cannot solve.

It is never too early to ask for professional help – this is the rule. When your finances are in trouble, seek help right away before it is too late. What is too late? If you only have one credit card, and you miss two months worth of payments, then it is advisable that you start consulting a professional who can at least advise you on helping manage your finances better. They will provide you with resources, workshops, courses and even support groups that you can attend.

If you have more than one credit card, even missing one month's payment can send you into a financial downward spiral that you may not be able to recover from.

You do not want to go down this road – harassing phone calls and the risk of getting bad credit to add to your stress levels.

Again, this is where having a financial goal is very important. Most people fall into the trap of believing that they will be able to catch up. They juggle money around from one credit card to another, and before they know it, it is too late. They no longer want to look into their credit card and bank accounts because they 'know' how bad it is, which makes it worse.

Seeking professional help is not about giving up or surrendering your credit cards; it is merely consulting with a professional who can give you objective advice and help get you back on track.

There is no need to be afraid as these services are strictly confidential. Your bank or creditors will not be made aware that you are seeking financial counseling, nor will they be notified of your financial situation.

Paid versus Free Credit Counseling

There are many agencies that offer 'free' credit counseling, but be careful as their services may not really be free. These private companies may offer you a free initial consultation, but to hire their services you need to pay a monthly fee.

If you are considering credit counseling, it is best to look for non-profit organizations offering credit counseling assistance. They offer their services for free or for a very minimal fee, depending on your financial capabilities.

The credit counselors working in these non-profit organizations also tend to be more sensitive to your needs, as they are really there to assist you in getting back on your feet.

The other thing that you also have to remember, is that once you sign-up with a private credit counseling firm and can no longer make the monthly payments, you will then be released and advised to seek assistance from a bankruptcy trustee. If you then seek the assistance from a non-profit credit counseling organization, it makes things a bit more complicated for them to assist you. Therefore, if you are in need of credit counseling, look for non-profit credit counseling organizations in your area first.

Chapter 21: Seeking Help From Professionals

Budget or credit counseling allows you to take control of your finances with the help of a professional budget or credit counsellor.

Anyone can get budget or credit counseling advice. These professionals will assist you in creating a realistic plan for managing your money, and help figure out other options that maybe budgeting alone cannot solve.

It is never too early to ask for professional help – this is the rule. When your finances are in trouble, seek help right away before it is too late. What is too late? If you only have one credit card, and you miss two months worth of payments, then it is advisable that you start consulting a professional who can at least advise you on helping manage your finances better. They will provide you with resources, workshops, courses and even support groups that you can attend.

If you have more than one credit card, even missing one month's payment can send you into a financial downward spiral that you may not be able to recover from.

You do not want to go down this road – harassing phone calls and the risk of getting bad credit to add to your stress levels.

Again, this is where having a financial goal is very important. Most people fall into the trap of believing that they will be able to catch up. They juggle money around from one credit card to another, and before they know it, it is too late. They no longer want to look into their credit card and bank accounts because they 'know' how bad it is, which makes it worse.

Seeking professional help is not about giving up or surrendering your credit cards; it is merely consulting with a professional who can give you objective advice and help get you back on track.

There is no need to be afraid as these services are strictly confidential. Your bank or creditors will not be made aware that you are seeking financial counseling, nor will they be notified of your financial situation.

Paid versus Free Credit Counseling

There are many agencies that offer 'free' credit counseling, but be careful as their services may not really be free. These private companies may offer you a free initial consultation, but to hire their services you need to pay a monthly fee.

If you are considering credit counseling, it is best to look for non-profit organizations offering credit counseling assistance. They offer their services for free or for a very minimal fee, depending on your financial capabilities.

The credit counselors working in these non-profit organizations also tend to be more sensitive to your needs, as they are really there to assist you in getting back on your feet.

The other thing that you also have to remember, is that once you sign-up with a private credit counseling firm and can no longer make the monthly payments, you will then be released and advised to seek assistance from a bankruptcy trustee. If you then seek the assistance from a non-profit credit counseling organization, it makes things a bit more complicated for them to assist you. Therefore, if you are in need of credit counseling, look for non-profit credit counseling organizations in your area first.

Chapter 22: What Are The Basic Elements Of A Budget?

Basic Elements of a Budget

The most ideal approach to get what you need in life is to set up an arrangement. Think about your own financial limit as that arrangement, representing the cash you have to go through every month while additionally giving you a little squirm space for that new application you simply need to download. A decent spending frameworks your needs, yet it additionally encourages you put some cash in a safe spot so you can accomplish your long haul monetary objectives. The measure of cash you decide to spend in a given zone is an individual choice, however the essential components of an individual spending plan are the equivalent.

Start With Your Income

The key component to any financial limit is salary. Without a standard wellspring of assets, there is no economical method to take care of tabs and make buys. For spending arranging and the executives purposes, your net gain, or salary, is the main pay that is significant in light of the fact that it's the main cash coming in that is spendable. On the off chance that you have different wellsprings of ordinary salary, add those to your spending limit also, however on the off chance that you have sporadic pay or rewards, you likely can't rely on those frequently enough to remember them for your month to month bookkeeping.

Proceed onward to Fixed Expenses

Fixed costs are charges that stay the equivalent from month to month. Your lease, vehicle installments and vehicle protection bills are normally a set sum over a set timeframe. This consistency makes fixed costs simple to represent in arranging and dealing with your financial limit.

Consider Flexible Expenses Next

Adaptable, or variable, costs change starting with one charging or spending period then onto the next. For instance, the electric bill might be $100 one month and $150 the following because of colder temperatures that caused an expanded requirement for heat. You may likewise burn through $25 on fuel multi week yet need $35 the following since you needed to go for a regular checkup. These adaptable costs can be evaluated and controlled with great spending propensities.

Remember Unplanned Expenses

Spontaneous costs are an essential component of any great spending plan. As indicated by money related creator Dave Ramsey, crises consistently emerge. By having reserves saved for managing startling occasions, for example, a punctured tire or a wrecked water radiator, you won't need to stray into the red or totally ruin your spending limit to manage the unexpected cost.

Increment Your General Savings

Every one of the specialists instruct you to pay yourself first, and that is the place investment funds come in. Put aside at least 10 percent of your salary before covering some other tabs and you'll rapidly wind up with a developing retirement fund. Clutch your investment funds for the long haul to support retirement, or let it work for momentary objectives, for example, getting away or purchasing another vehicle.

Little Business»Business Planning and Strategy»Sales Forecasting»

What Are the Essential Parts of Developing a Budget?

What Will Happen if an Organization Does Not Properly Budget?

Business Budgeting Tools

Money Forecasting Tools

Planning Process Improvements and Recommendations

Business spending plans ought to be dynamic budgetary records that help control your basic leadership consistently. Notwithstanding an essential rundown of assessed incomes and costs, spending plans ought to contain recipes that help show projections. Understanding the essential components of an independent venture spending will assist you with making one that causes you keep your business on track from month to month.

Income Forecasting

One of the most basic pieces of the spending procedure is anticipating your business incomes. While you may have unpredictable incomes, for example, benefits from ventures or the clearance of advantages, knowing your center income streams will assist you with framing the establishment of your financial limit. Utilize verifiable deals information, overviews of clients and projections from your business staff to appraise your incomes as precisely as would be prudent. Create preservationist and hopeful projections to assist you with arranging spending plans that address the two situations.

Cost Estimates

When you have a smart thought of your income, you can all the more precisely set cost levels. Separating your expenses into creation and overhead costs is a key piece of building up a business spending plan. Generation costs are those identified with making your item or administration, while overhead expenses are those you have in any event, when you aren't making what you sell. Instances of generation costs incorporate materials and work, while overhead costs incorporate promoting, lease and telephones.

Obligation Service

On the off chance that you utilize a Visa or advances to work your business, remember to incorporate your month to month intrigue charges. Neglecting to extend how a lot of intrigue you'll produce during the year can prompt incorrect year-end projections and an absence of credit. For instance, in the event that you produce $200 worth of intrigue every month that is attached onto your Visa balance, add that to your month to month planned costs. On the off chance that you don't, at that point by November you will have $2,000 less credit accessible than your spending appears.

Income Projections

Entrepreneurs frequently wrongly create spending plans that show pay and costs, however not when they show up or come due. This can cause income issues that harm your business. Make an income report as a major aspect of your lord spending that shows when your business cash will show up, not exactly when it's reserved. Incorporate the dates you'll need to take care of tabs, not exactly when you collect these costs. For instance, if a client orders $10,000 worth of item from you in January, you probably won't get installment until March. You may need to pay your providers and laborers for the materials and work vital for that request in February.

Projections

A fundamental piece of making any financial limit is including equations that task long haul pay and costs. For instance, your spending archive will record your month to month incredibly in every month except ought to likewise assess your normal costs every month as you update your numbers. This will show your assessed last yearly cost at these levels. Make recipes that let you rapidly locate your normal month to month pay and costs and year-end projections.

3 Essential Elements of a Budget: People, Data, Process

For any association, a financial limit, regardless of whether done every year or led during the time through moving figures, is a basic part for progress. Any fruitful spending plan must associate three significant components – individuals, information and procedure. A breakdown in any of these regions can majorly affect your outcomes. How would you unite the 3 basic components of a financial limit?

Here are a few hints Individuals

A spending limit can't be made, at its very establishment, by anybody however a person. Your kin are fundamental. An unengaged individual, or one who isn't responsible, is probably going to make an unacceptable spending plan. How would you keep them associated? Make a point to, right off the bat, give thinking behind the assignment. On the off chance that they comprehend the significance of the financial limit, and their job in making it, you at that point give them inspiration to give precise commitments dependent on exertion. Give them an opportunity to manufacture a quality spending plan – don't simply give them a format without course and anticipate that them should discover time in their calendar to finish it.

Information

Clearly information is similarly as significant as the human component – you can't make a financial limit without crude numbers. There are a few sub-components that are key here, in particular detail – attempt to catch however much detail as could be expected, drivers – analyze everything that drives your

income, outer data – give any outside data that may be valuable to the benefactors or analysts, and practicality – ensure information is as modern as could be expected under the circumstances.

Procedure

When you have your kin and your information, your procedure unites everything. A procedure that is unyielding or obsolete methods your final product will probably be shoddy. There are a few factors that help to consummate a procedure. For instance, how effectively can the individuals included access the framework, information and parts they have to carry out their responsibility? How secure is the data? How regularly are the numbers being assessed/revised? A procedure that ensures that these components are tended to will prompt a spending that reflects current patterns and current organization assets and expectations.

With regards to planning and gauging, guaranteeing that these 3 basic components of a spending work in complete attachment is the best way to gather genuine monetary truth. You can't anticipate that one should

work without the other two – you need each of the three to accomplish a perfect business spending plan.

Chapter 23 Have An Open And Generous Attitude

By this time, you should have already learned that saving money is crucial. However, this does not mean that you should focus solely on saving. If you want to live a good life, you should also learn how to give. There is a saying that you make a living by what you get, but you make a life by what you give. If you will read the Bible, you will not find anything that says tithing is expected or applicable in today's time. Tithing was an old system brought about by the people's exodus from Egypt as well as the forming of a new nation. This nation was divided into twelve tribes, with eleven of them growing crops and raising animals. The last tribe, where Levi belonged to, had no crops, animals and land, so the other eleven tribes had to give them ten percent of what they have. In today's time, tithing is no longer applicable. Nevertheless, it is still encouraged. Do not worry because nothing bad will happen to you if you do not tithe. You are not obligated to do it. People are encouraged to tithe for their own benefit. Through tithing and giving to the church or any other charity, you can practice generosity and develop a giving or abundance mindset. You learn to be selfless.

Selfless people tend to be more successful in life because they get along better with others and they remain optimistic despite adversity. Because of their positive attitude, they can achieve their goals and even help other people in achieving theirs. When you tithe, you do not only offer money to the church or charity, but you also allow yourself to develop a positive attitude.

How about taxes? Can you count your tithes on your tax returns? Yes, you can! This is such good news for taxpayers. Do not worry because the value and sanctity of your offering does not diminish when you take the tax deduction. Once you get your tax refund, you can give it if you want.

Chapter 24: How To Reduce Your Spending

After you've figured out where your money is going each month and you've built a workable budget, you will probably still want to reduce spending in a few categories. It's pretty rare for a person to decide they don't want to save more money, whether it's for a house, a trip, or a rainy day. How can you cut down on your spending? There are lots of strategies.

Decide how much money you want to save

The first step is to think about your goals and decide how much money you want to save each month. Do you have a big trip coming up within the year and the quarter jar isn't going to cut it? Maybe saving $20 per month somewhere will get you the vacation you want. Maybe you want to start paying off some debts faster and you need to trim that cash from your budget.

That could mean reducing your spending by less than $20, but it's a more long-term strategy than saving for a trip, so you ultimately save more to pay off debts. Think about how much money exactly you want (or need) to save. This will give you a clearer idea of what will need to change in your life and spending habits.

Try a spending freeze

A "spending freeze" is a bold way to reduce your spending in one fell swoop. The idea is that you don't spend any money for a certain period of time. It can be a good tactic if you're trying to balance out your budgeting sheet or saving up for something. There are stories out there of people who've gone weeks or even a month in a spending freeze. That's pretty unpractical for most, so if you decide to try it, pick a reasonable time frame. Maybe commit to one weekend per month for your freeze, and count up how much money that saves you. You can also decide to freeze just one or two categories, like entertainment and groceries, for the time period you've selected.

Take a closer look at your budget categories

Look at your budget categories and the amount of money dedicated to each one. Some of the categories, like health insurance or car payments, are probably not super flexible. That doesn't mean there aren't ways to save money, but right now, we're going to focus on the categories where it's much easier to cut down. Look at the entertainment or food sections. Do the numbers seem high? Do you believe you could make some changes to spend less? Identify the categories you believe have extra fat and focus on those.

Take steps to cut spending in specific categories

You know the categories you're going to cut, but how do you go about doing that? Let's take a look at three of the most common categories where people reduce their spending: entertainment, food, and utilities.

Entertainment

This category can include things like going to movies, going out to eat, renting DVDs, going to concerts, paying for cable and streaming services, buying video games, buying books, and so on. For some people, travel might also be included in this section, or they might put eating out in their food budget. It's up to you. Depending on how much you spend on entertainment, it can be fairly easy to reduce your spending. Here's how:

Pay for just one streaming subscription

There are lots of streaming services available now, each costing as little as $7 up to $15, though other add-ons like Hulu's access to live TV increases the price significantly. How many services are you paying for? Think about which one you actually use the most. Always turning to Netflix's movies and TV shows, while only watching one thing on Hulu? Consider sacrificing that one show and cut spending.

Keep in mind when we say "streaming services," we aren't counting Amazon, because streaming is included with Amazon Prime, which itself saves tons of money on shipping. However, if you never actually buy anything from Amazon, but pay for Amazon Prime to get the streaming TV, you can lump that in with other services while choosing which one you want.

Look for free entertainment

Fun doesn't have to be expensive. If you like going out and having new experiences, you don't have to pay a lot, or even anything. Depending on the area you live in, there could be tons of options like free music events and art fairs, while places that normally charge an admission (like museums or zoos) frequently have discount or even free days. If you live in an area with lots of parks, take up hiking, walking, or biking. This is a great way to enjoy nature and get in better shape.

Get a library card

The library counts as "free entertainment," but it's a significant-enough step to get its own section. Getting a library card is super easy, always free, and depending on how stocked your library system is, you can get access to books, movies, and sometimes even video games. If you love books, you know how expensive they can get, especially if you're buying physical copies. Get them from the library instead and if you really love one, then you can buy it. Getting movies from the library can replace going to a movie at a theater, which can be very pricey, especially if you're paying for a family. You'll have to wait a while to see new releases, but if you just can't wait for a specific film, consider at least waiting until it comes out on RedBox. It will still be way cheaper than paying for a theater.

Only buy used electronics/books/games/movies/etc

If you are a gadget lover, book lover, gamer, or film buff, you might spend a lot of cash on your hobby. Video games and gadgets can be especially expensive. Thankfully, you don't necessarily have to stop buying things altogether to save money. Instead, commit to buying only used items. Click on the little "new and used" button on Amazon below the main price, and find a cheaper version of what you're looking for. You can also see the reviews for the seller and they will (frequently) give a description of the used item's condition.

Other shopping options include Facebook Market, Ebay, thrift stores, Goodwill, Craigslist, and more. Always exercise caution when buying stuff used. You should always ideally get to inspect the item before buying, though if you're going online, you probably won't get to do this. You'll have to just rely on seller reviews.

Food/grocery

Everyone has to eat, but you can reduce your spending in this section by making different choices. It sometimes takes a bit more effort and intention, but if it allows you to save more money, it's worth it.

Research grocery stores and find the one with the best prices

Are you shopping at an expensive grocery store like Whole Foods? Maybe you aren't, but you think there might still be a cheaper store out there. Do some research on stores that offer the best deals and consider switching, at least for items you buy a lot. This may seem a matter of just a few dollars, but it adds up quickly. If you really love your grocery store or it's really the only one that's convenient, look at how many name brands you're buying and switch to the generic. Most of the time, there isn't much of a difference. If you really dislike the generic version of a food item, don't feel pressured to get it. You should get what you like, but odds are, there will be at least a few grocery items you can swap out for a cheaper variation.

Cook more at home

If you count going out to restaurants as part of your food budget, check out how much money you're spending per month. Maybe you only go out to a few times, but you're going to places with high price tags. Or, maybe you get fast food or some other cheaper option, but it's a twice-weekly thing. Commit to eating out less and cooking more at home.

Find recipes for simple meals that only use a handful of ingredients; you want the cooking to be easy, or it will be challenging to stick to your new goal. It's also a good idea to find recipes that work really well as leftovers, so you can really stretch the ingredients and get the most value possible out of them. You don't have to give up eating out altogether, but by replacing some of those meals with home-cooked ones, you definitely will see the difference in your wallet.

Get really good at using coupons and finding sales

There's no reason why you shouldn't be using coupons for some of your essential kitchen staples. Clipping coupons seems like an outdated habit, but money is money, and just about every grocery store big and small still offers coupons. You can find ones online, too, often from specific brands on their website. Commit to remembering to bring coupons with you when you shop and adjusting your grocery list based on the coupons you have. If the coupon is for a different brand than you usually use, use it anyway. It's just one time; if you hate the different brand, just don't buy it again.

You should also always be on the lookout for sales. "Buy one, get one free" sales are really great, especially for items you use a lot, like olive oil, mayo, cereal, cleaning products, and so on. If you never eat the item that's on sale, don't feel obligated to pick it up. If you don't like it and never get around to the second item, you didn't really save any money.

Consider a wholesale store like Costco

Stores like Costco let you buy items in bulk, so you pay significantly less over time. However, you do have to pay a membership, so think about if it's worth it or not. As an example, a family of just two people will probably not get through the enormous volume of items fast enough to really make the membership cost worth it. A family of four or more, however, is much more likely to save money in the long-run. Unfortunately, you can't share memberships with just anyone; they have to be a spouse, domestic partner, or child under 18-years who lives in your home. If you don't want to buy a membership, however, you can have a friend with a membership buy a Costco cash card. These have no expiration date and hold between $25-$1,000. While only members can buy or add money to these cards, nonmembers can use them. You just pay your friend the amount you want added on the card, and then you're free to go shopping!

Utilities

Utilities include water, electricity, and air conditioning or heating. If you take a look at your bills, you know you're probably paying more than you would like. Luckily, it's fairly easy to reduce your spending without drastically changing your lifestyle.

Unplug devices you aren't using

One of the simplest ways to save money on electricity is to just unplug devices when you aren't using them. "Phantom" loads or "phantom" charges account for around 10% of your electric bill per month, according a study by the EPA and other agencies. Keep track of your various devices like cell phone chargers, lamps, computers, and power cords. When you aren't using them, just disconnect them. This is especially important when you go on vacation; you don't want all your devices sucking energy for a week or more while you aren't even home.

Change to more efficient light bulbs

Another easy way to save on your electric bill is to switch your bulbs. CFLs or LEDs are around four times more efficient than traditional incandescent bulbs. They also last longer. Look at the lumens number, not the wattage, when comparing bulbs. When you switch a normal 60-watt with a 14-watt LED, you only save around $0.66 a month on that one bulb, but if you replace a whole bunch, that adds up over the course of a year.

Get a programmable thermostat

Most of us need to heat our homes in the winter and cool them down in the summer. However, blasting either hot or cold air constantly will cause your bill to skyrocket. By getting a programmable thermostat, you can adjust settings so the cooling or heating starts and stops at certain times. In the winter, adjust the thermostat so the heat is off while you're at work, but starts when you're about an hour from coming back home, so you come home to a comfortable temperature. In the summer, set the air conditioning to run while you're home during the day, but then have it turn off at night when the air gets cooler.

Lower the hot temperature on your water heater

Most people have their hot water heater set higher than necessary. That heating can make up 14% of your energy costs per month. To reduce spending, adjust the temperature down. You can also install a water heater blanket or insulate exposed hot water pipes to keep them from losing heat. It's more efficient and saves you money. Most experts recommend a range of a 120-140 degrees. You can adjust the heater yourself, but many don't have numbered dials, so you're guessing what the temperature is. A simple way to figure what your heater is currently set to is run the hot water out of your tap for a while, fill a glass, and use a thermometer to see what it is. Adjust the dial and do another test. There are lots of how-to's online that give more detailed instructions on lowering your water heater's temp.

Chapter 25: Ways You Can Adapt To Save Money

Saving money is a difficult task for most of the people because fund saving needs proper management of all the processes taking place with money. All the entrepreneurs and the trades, businesses require proper money management. Saving cash is mainly concerned with proper money management. If there is no management system in any entrepreneur or any business, then no money can be saved.

Money management:

There are so many things which are included in funds management, some of them are explained below.

Investment:

When we come to the investment, it means that we are spending funds on some tasks, either we will face profit and success, or we will have to face a loss? These two things should be kept in mind whenever you are about to invest money, so invest only that amount of cash which on the loss you can recover.

Budgeting:

Budgeting means to set up or to plan expenditure within the amount in hands. So if you set your budget in limits of money, then you probably can save lots of money.

Taxation:

Taxation is also included in money management, means when you are setting up the money management level, you can't ignore taxes, because you have to give them at any cost. And if you set your goals including taxes then you probably can save a lot of money.

Banking:

Proper banking can also save your money, means while setting your money plans you have to give a look on its banking too, just because if your banking is not proper then you can face lots of money problems.

All the above things cannot be ignored while you set your goals for saving cash, each of them has its importance.

Cash flow in business:

Lots of funds problems are seen in businesses since not every person can run a business successfully. A business needs the talent of money management. Regardless of the way someone runs a business, if the financial plans are poor, they will face losses and hence little to no money can be made. Instead, money will be lost and the business ruined.

Even a small business owner also worries about his money and cash flow problems. The amount of cash coming into a company refers to to profits. How much is going out of the business refers to losses. This cash flow problem can easily be solved by making cash flow charts and giving each step as much importance as it needs. This means that in a business, proper budgeting and money investment programs should be there. Otherwise, companies can face big losses.

Apart from your business, money management systems are also required at home. Partners can make money plans together so that they don't have to face money problems. Everywhere, saving money needs proper money management. Otherwise no money can be saved.

Conclusion

Thank you again for downloading this book. I hope this book was able to help you budget your money. A lot of people tend to find that budgeting their money is not something that they are able to do easily. This is not because budgeting your money is a task that is near impossible, it is simply that people go about it in the wrong way. If you want to make the most out of your current financial situation and your future financial situation, you are going to want to make sure that you are carefully reviewing all of your options.

When you are budgeting money, it is important to make sure that you are allowing yourself to have a little extra money each month for a fun activity. No matter what that activity is, you want to budget it in. You might think that budgeting your money means cutting out all of the extras. However, the best way to budget is to cut out MOST of the extras, find ways to decrease the cost of the "must pays" and allow yourself a little fun money. If you deprive yourself and your family of any extras, you will eventually crack and end up spending the electric bill money on a night out. This is not a great way to go about budgeting your money. Budgeting money means thinking ahead and doing your best to avoid future problems.

Now, when it comes to actually sitting down to budget everything, you might think that you have it under control. However, if this is all new to you, there might be some key things you could be doing that you will simply miss out on. You want to make sure that you are giving yourself the best shot possible at making this work to your own advantage. The best way to do that is to go ahead and seek professional help in budgeting your money. Don't worry about being embarrassed. There is a reason such services are out there. They are professionals and they have been doing this much longer than you. Budgeting money with the help of professionals is the best route to go. Of course, you want to make sure that you are selecting the best of the best when it comes to such assistance. This way, you will not have to worry about whether or not you are truly going to be able to be a success with this venture. Get started now and before you know it, you will have made your financial situation so much better.

Thank you and good luck!